Sonnets by Michael Drayton

Michael Drayton was born in 1563 at Hartshill, near Nuneaton, Warwickshire, England. The facts of his early life remain unknown.

Drayton first published, in 1590, a volume of spiritual poems; The Harmony of the Church. Ironically the Archbishop of Canterbury seized almost the entire edition and had it destroyed.

In 1593 he published Idea: The Shepherd's Garland, 9 pastorals celebrating his own love-sorrows under the poetic name of Rowland. This was later expanded to a 64 sonnet cycle.

With the publication of The Legend of Piers Gaveston, Matilda and Mortimeriados, later enlarged and re-published, in 1603, under the title of The Barons' Wars. His career began to gather interest and attention.

In 1596, The Legend of Robert, Duke of Normandy, another historical poem was published, followed in 1597 by England's Heroical Epistles, a series of historical studies, in imitation of those of Ovid. Written in the heroic couplet, they contain some of his finest writing.

Like other poets of his era, Drayton wrote for the theatre; but unlike Shakespeare, Jonson, or Samuel Daniel, he invested little of his art in the genre. Between 1597 and 1602, Drayton was a member of the stable of playwrights who worked for Philip Henslowe. Henslowe's Diary links Drayton's name with 23 plays from that period, and, for all but one unfinished work, in collaboration with others such as Thomas Dekker, Anthony Munday, and Henry Chettle. Only one play has survived; Part 1 of Sir John Oldcastle, which Drayton wrote with Munday, Robert Wilson, and Richard Hathwaye but little of Drayton can be seen in its pages.

By this time, as a poet, Drayton was well received and admired at the Court of Elizabeth 1st. If he hoped to continue that admiration with the accession of James 1st he thought wrong. In 1603, he addressed a poem of compliment to James I, but it was ridiculed, and his services rudely rejected.

In 1605 Drayton reprinted his most important works; the historical poems and the Idea. Also published was a fantastic satire called The Man in the Moon and, for the for the first time the famous Ballad of Agincourt.

Since 1598 he had worked on Poly-Olbion, a work to celebrate all the points of topographical or antiquarian interest in Great Britain. Eighteen books in total, the first were published in 1614 and the last in 1622.

In 1627 he published another of his miscellaneous volumes. In it Drayton printed The Battle of Agincourt (an historical poem but not to be confused with his ballad on the same subject), The Miseries of Queen Margaret, and the acclaimed Nimphidia, the Court of Faery, as well as several other important pieces.

Drayton last published in 1630 with The Muses' Elizium.

Michael Drayton died in London on December 23rd, 1631. He was buried in Westminster Abbey, in Poets' Corner. A monument was placed there with memorial lines attributed to Ben Jonson.

Index of Contents

SONNETS FROM THE 1594 EDITION

TO THE DEERE CHYLD OF THE MUSES, AND HIS EVER KIND MECÆNAS, MASTER ANTHONY COOKE, ESQ

Vovchsafe to grace these rude vnpolish'd rymes,
Which long (dear friend) haue slept in sable night,
And, come abroad now in these glorious tymes,
Can hardly brook the purenes of the light.
But still you see their desteny is such,
That in the world theyr fortune they must try,
Perhaps they better shall abide the tuch,
Wearing your name, theyr gracious liuery.
Yet these mine owne: I wrong not other men,
Nor trafique further then thys happy Clyme,
Nor filch from Portes, nor from Petrarchs pen,
A fault too common in this latter time.
Divine Syr Phillip, I auouch thy writ,
I am no Pickpurse of anothers wit.
Yours devoted,
M. DRAYTON.

AMOUR I

Reade heere (sweet Mayd) the story of my wo,
The drery abstracts of my endles cares,
With my lives sorow enterlyned so;
Smok'd with my sighes, and blotted with my teares:
The sad memorials of my miseries,

Pend in the griefe of myne afflicted ghost;
My lives complaint in doleful Elegies,
With so pure love as tyme could never boast.
Receaue the incense which I offer heere,
By my strong fayth ascending to thy fame,
My zeale, my hope, my vowes, my praise, my prayer,
My soules oblation to thy sacred name:
Which name my Muse to highest heaven shal raise
By chast desire, true love, and vertues praise.

AMOUR II

My fayre, if thou wilt register my love,
More then worlds volumes shall thereof arise;
Preserve my teares, and thou thy selfe shall prove
A second flood downe rayning from mine eyes.
Note but my sighes, and thine eyes shal behold
The Sun-beames smothered with immortall smoke;
And if by thee, my prayers may be enrold,
They heaven and earth to pitty shall provoke.
Looke thou into my breast, and thou shall see
Chaste holy vowes for my soules sacrifice:
That soule (sweet Maide) which so hath honoured thee,
Erecting Trophies to thy sacred eyes;
Those eyes to my heart shining ever bright,
When darknes hath obscur'd each other light.

AMOUR III

My thoughts bred up with Eagle-birds of love,
And, for their vertues I desiered to know,
Upon the nest I set them forth, to prove
If they were of the Eagles kinde or no:
But they no sooner saw my Sunne appeare,
But on her rayes with gazing eyes they stood;
Which proov'd my birds delighted in the ayre,
And that they came of this rare kinglie brood.
But now their plumes, full sumd with sweet desire,
To shew their kinde began to clime the skies:
Doe what I could my Eaglets would aspire,
Straight mounting up to thy celestiall eyes.
And thus (my faire) my thoughts away be flowne,
And from my breast into thine eyes be gone.

AMOUR IV

My faire, had I not erst adorned my Lute
With those sweet strings stolne from thy golden hayre,
Vnto the world had all my joyes been mute,
Nor had I learn'd to descant on my faire.
Had not mine eye seene thy Celestiall eye,
Nor my hart knowne the power of thy name,
My soule had ne'er felt thy Divinitie,
Nor my Muse been the trumpet of thy fame.
But thy divine perfections, by their skill,
This miracle on my poore Muse have tried,
And, by inspiring, glorifide my quill,
And in my verse thy selfe art deified:
Thus from thy selfe the cause is thus derived,
That by thy fame all fame shall be survived.

AMOUR V

Since holy Vestall lawes have been neglected,
The Gods pure fire hath been extinguisht quite;
No Virgin once attending on that light,
Nor yet those heavenly secrets once respected;
Till thou alone, to pay the heavens their dutie
Within the Temple of thy sacred name,
With thine eyes kindling that Celestiall flame,
By those reflecting Sun-beames of thy beautie.
Here Chastity that Vestall most divine,
Attends that Lampe with eye which never sleepeth;
The volumes of Religions lawes shee keepeth,
Making thy breast that sacred reliques shryne,
Where blessed Angels, singing day and night,
Praise him which made that fire, which lends that light.

AMOUR VI

In one whole world is but one Phoenix found,
A Phoenix thou, this Phoenix then alone:
By thy rare plume thy kind is easly knowne,
With heavenly colours dide, with natures wonder cround.
Heape thine own vertues, seasoned by their sunne,
On heavenly top of thy divine desire;
Then with thy beautie set the same on fire,
So by thy death thy life shall be begunne.
Thy selfe, thus burned in this sacred flame,
With thine owne sweetnes all the heavens perfuming,
And stil increasing as thou art consuming,

Shalt spring againe from th' ashes of thy fame;
And mounting up shall to the heavens ascend:
So maist thou live, past world, past fame, past end.

AMOUR VII

Stay, stay, sweet Time; behold, or ere thou passe
From world to world, thou long hast sought to see,
That wonder now wherein all wonders be,
Where heaven beholds her in a mortall glasse.
Nay, looke thee, Time, in this Celesteall glasse,
And thy youth past in this faire mirror see:
Behold worlds Beautie in her infancie,
What shee was then, and thou, or ere shee was.
Now passe on, Time: to after-worlds tell this,
Tell truelie, Time, what in thy time hath beene,
That they may tel more worlds what Time hath seene,
And heaven may joy to think on past worlds blisse.
Heere make a Period, Time, and saie for mee,
She was the like that never was, nor never more shalbe.

AMOUR VIII

Unto the World, to Learning, and to Heaven,
Three nines there are, to everie one a nine;
One number of the earth, the other both divine,
One wonder woman now makes three od numbers even.
Nine orders, first, of Angels be in heaven;
Nine Muses doe with learning still frequent:
These with the Gods are ever resident.
Nine worthy men vnto the world were given.
My Worthie one to these nine Worthies addeth,
And my faire Muse one Muse vnto the nine;
And my good Angell, in my soule divine,
With one more order these nine orders gladdeth.
My Muse, my Worthy, and my Angell, then,
Makes every one of these three nines a ten.

AMOUR IX

Beauty sometime, in all her glory crowned,
Passing by that cleere fountain of thine eye,
Her sun-shine face there chaunsing to espy,
Forgot herselfe, and thought she had been drowned.
And thus, whilst Beautie on her beauty gazed,

Who then, yet living, deemd she had been dying,
And yet in death some hope of life espying,
At her owne rare perfections so amazed;
Twixt joy and griefe, yet with a smyling frowning,
The glorious sun-beames of her eyes bright shining,
And shee, in her owne destiny divining,
Threw in herselfe, to save herselfe by drowning;
The Well of Nectar, pav'd with pearle and gold,
Where shee remaines for all eyes to behold.

AMOUR X

Oft taking pen in hand, with words to cast my woes,
Beginning to account the sum of all my cares,
I well perceive my griefe innumerable growes,
And still in reckonings rise more millions of dispayres.
And thus, deviding of my fatall howres,
The payments of my love I read, and reading crosse,
And in substracting set my sweets vnto my sowres;
Th' average of my joyes directs me to my losse.
And thus mine eyes, a debtor to thine eye,
Who by extortion gaineth all theyr lookes,
My hart hath payd such grievous usury,
That all her wealth lyes in thy Beauties bookes;
And all is thine which hath been due to mee,
And I a Banckrupt, quite undone by thee.

AMOUR XI

Thine eyes taught mee the Alphabet of love,
To con my Cros-rowe ere I learn'd to spell;
For I was apt, a scholler like to prove,
Gave mee sweet lookes when as I learned well.
Vowes were my vowels, when I then begun
At my first Lesson in thy sacred name:
My consonants the next when I had done,
Words consonant, and sounding to thy fame.
My liquids then were liquid christall teares,
My cares my mutes, so mute to crave reliefe;
My dolefull Dypthongs were my lives dispaires,
Redoubling sighes the accents of my griefe:
My loves Schoole-mistris now hath taught me so,
That I can read a story of my woe.

AMOUR XII

Some Atheist or vile Infidell in love,
When I doe speake of thy divinitie,
May blaspheme thus, and say I flatter thee,
And onely write my skill in verse to prove.
See myracles, ye unbeleeving! see
A dumbe-born Muse made to expresse the mind,
A cripple hand to write, yet lame by kind,
One by thy name, the other touching thee.
Blind were mine eyes, till they were seene of thine,
And mine eares deafe by thy fame healed be;
My vices cur'd by vertues sprung from thee,
My hopes reviu'd, which long in grave had lyne:
All vncleane thoughts, foule spirits, cast out in mee
By thy great power, and by strong fayth in thee.

AMOUR XIII

Cleere Ankor, on whose silver-sanded shore
My soule-shrinde Saint, my faire Idea, lyes;
O blessed Brooke! whose milk-white Swans adore
The christall streame refined by her eyes:
Where sweet Myrh-breathing Zephyre in the spring
Gently distils his Nectar-dropping showers;
Where Nightingales in Arden sit and sing
Amongst those dainty dew-empearled flowers.
Say thus, fayre Brooke, when thou shall see thy Queene:
Loe! heere thy Shepheard spent his wandring yeeres,
And in these shades (deer Nimphe) he oft hath been,
And heere to thee he sacrifiz'd his teares.
Fayre Arden, thou my Tempe art alone,
And thou, sweet Ankor, art my Helicon.

AMOUR XIV

Looking into the glasse of my youths miseries,
I see the ugly face of my deformed cares,
With withered browes, all wrinckled with dispaires,
That for my mis-spent youth the tears fel from my eyes.
Then, in these teares, the mirror of these eyes,
Thy fayrest youth and Beautie doe I see
Imprinted in my teares by looking still on thee:
Thus midst a thousand woes ten thousand joyes arise.
Yet in those joyes, the shadowes of my good,
In this fayre limned ground as white as snow,
Paynted the blackest Image of my woe,

With murthering hands imbru'd in mine own blood:
And in this Image his darke clowdy eyes,
My life, my youth, my love, I heere Anotamize.

AMOUR XV

Now, Love, if thou wilt prove a Conqueror,
Subdue thys Tyrant ever martyring mee;
And but appoint me for her Tormentor,
Then for a Monarch will I honour thee.
My hart shall be the prison for my fayre;
Ile fetter her in chaines of purest love,
My sighs shall stop the passage of the ayre:
This punishment the pittilesse may move.
With teares out of the Channels of mine eyes
She'st quench her thirst as duly as they fall:
Kinde words vnkindest meate I can devise,
My sweet, my faire, my good, my best of all.
Ile binde her then with my torne-tressed haire,
And racke her with a thousand holy wishes;
Then, on a place prepared for her there,
Ile execute her with a thousand kisses.
Thus will I crucifie, my cruell shee;
Thus Ile plague her which hath so plagued mee.

AMOUR XVI

Vertues Idea in virginitie,
By inspiration, came conceav'd with thought:
The time is come delivered she must be,
Where first my love into the world was brought.
Vnhappy borne, of all unhappy day!
So luckles was my Babes nativity,
Saturne chiefe Lord of the Ascendant lay,
The wandring Moone in earths triplicitie.
Now, or by chaunce or heavens hie providence,
His Mother died, and by her Legacie
(Fearing the stars presaging influence)
Bequeath'd his wardship to my soueraignes eye;
Where hunger-starven, wanting lookes to live,
Still empty gorg'd, with cares consumption pynde,
Salt luke-warm teares shee for his drink did give,
And ever-more with sighes he supt and dynde:
And thus (poore Orphan) lying in distresse
Cryes in his pangs, God helpe the motherlesse.

AMOUR XVII

If ever wonder could report a wonder,
Or tongue of wonder worth could tell a wonder thought,
Or ever joy expresse what perfect joy hath taught,
Then wonder, tongue, then joy, might wel report a wonder.
Could all conceite conclude, which past conceit admireth,
Or could mine eye but ayme her obiects past perfection,
My words might imitate my deerest thoughts direction,
And my soule then obtaine which so my soule desireth.
Were not Invention stauld, treading Inventions maze,
Or my swift-winged Muse tyred by too hie flying;
Did not perfection still on her perfection gaze,
Whilst Love (my Phoenix bird) in her owne flame is dying,
Invention and my Muse, perfection and her love,
Should teach the world to know the wonder that I prove.

AMOUR XVIII

Some, when in ryme they of their Loves doe tell,
With flames and lightning their exordiums paynt:
Some invocate the Gods, some spirits of Hell,
And heaven, and earth doe with their woes acquaint.
Elizia is too hie a seate for mee:
I wyll not come in Stixe or Phlegiton;
The Muses nice, the Furies cruell be,
I lyke not Limbo, nor blacke Acheron,
Spightful Erinnis frights mee with her lookes,
My manhood dares not with foule Ate mell:
I quake to looke on Hecats charming bookes,
I styll feare bugbeares in Apollos cell.
I passe not for Minerva nor Astræa.
But ever call upon divine Idea.

AMOUR XIX

If those ten Regions, registred by Fame,
By there ten Sibils have the world controld,
Who prophecied of Christ or ere he came,
And of his blessed birth before fore-told;
That man-god now, of whom they did divine,
This earth of those sweet Prophets hath bereft,
And since the world to judgement doth declyne,
Instead of ten, one Sibil to us left.
Thys pure Idea, vertues right Idea,

Shee of whom Merlin long tyme did fore-tell,
Excelling her of Delphos or Cumæa,
Whose lyfe doth save a thousand soules from hell:
That life (I meane) which doth Religion teach,
And by example true repentance preach.

AMOUR XX

Reading sometyme, my sorrowes to beguile,
I find old Poets hylls and floods admire:
One, he doth wonder monster-breeding Nyle,
Another meruailes Sulphure Aetnas fire.
Now broad-brymd Indus, then of Pindus height,
Pelion and Ossa, frosty Caucase old,
The Delian Cynthus, then Olympus weight,
Slow Arrer, franticke Gallus, Cydnus cold.
Some Ganges, Ister, and of Tagus tell,
Some whir-poole Po, and slyding Hypasis;
Some old Pernassus where the Muses dwell,
Some Helycon, and some faire Simois:
A, fooles! thinke I, had you Idea seene,
Poore Brookes and Banks had no such wonders beene.

AMOUR XXI

Letters and lynes, we see, are soone defaced,
Mettles doe waste and fret with cankers rust;
The Diamond shall once consume to dust,
And freshest colours with foule staines disgraced.
Paper and yncke can paynt but naked words,
To write with blood of force offends the sight,
And if with teares, I find them all too light;
And sighes and signes a silly hope affoords.
O, sweetest shadow! how thou seru'st my turne,
Which still shalt be as long as there is Sunne,
Nor whilst the world is never shall be done,
Whilst Moone shall shyne by night, or any fire shall burne:
That every thing whence shadow doth proceede,
May in his shadow my Loves story reade.

AMOUR XXII

My hart, imprisoned in a hopeless Ile,
Peopled with Armies of pale jealous eyes,
The shores beset with thousand secret spyes,

Must passe by ayre, or else dye in exile.
He framd him wings with feathers of his thought,
Which by theyr nature learn'd to mount the skye;
And with the same he practised to flye,
Till he himself thys Eagles art had taught.
Thus soring still, not looking once below,
So neere thyne eyes celesteall sunne aspyred,
That with the rayes his wafting pyneons fired:
Thus was the wanton cause of his owne woe.
Downe fell he, in thy Beauties Ocean drenched,
Yet there he burnes in fire thats never quenched.

AMOUR XXIII

Wonder of Heaven, glasse of divinitie,
Rare beautie, Natures joy, perfections Mother,
The worke of that vnited Trinitie,
Wherein each fayrest part excelleth other!
Loves Mithridate, the purest of perfection,
Celestiall Image, Load-stone of desire,
The soules delight, the sences true direction,
Sunne of the world, thou hart reuyuing fire!
Why should'st thou place thy Trophies in those eyes,
Which scorne the honor that is done to thee,
Or make my pen her name immortalize,
Who in her pride sdaynes once to look on me?
It is thy heaven within her face to dwell,
And in thy heaven, there onely, is my hell.

AMOUR XXIV

Our floods-Queene, Thames, for shyps and Swans is crowned,
And stately Severne for her shores is praised,
The christall Trent for Foords and fishe renowned,
And Avons fame to Albyons Clives is raysed.
Carlegion Chester vaunts her holy Dee,
Yorke many wonders of her Ouse can tell,
The Peake her Dove, whose bancks so fertill bee,
And Kent will say her Medway doth excell.
Cotswoold commends her Isis and her Tame,
Our Northern borders boast of Tweeds faire flood;
Our Westerne parts extoll theyr Wilys fame,
And old Legea brags of Danish blood:
Ardens sweet Ankor, let thy glory be
That fayre Idea shee doth live by thee.

AMOUR XXV

The glorious sunne went blushing to his bed,
When my soules sunne, from her fayre Cabynet,
Her golden beames had now discovered,
Lightning the world, eclipsed by his set.
Some muz'd to see the earth envy the ayre,
Which from her lyps exhald refined sweet,
A world to see, yet how he joyd to heare
The dainty grasse make musicke with her feete.
But my most meruaile was when from the skyes,
So Comet-like, each starre advanc'd her lyght,
As though the heaven had now awak'd her eyes,
And summond Angels to this blessed sight.
No clowde was seene, but christalline the ayre,
Laughing for joy upon my lovely fayre.

AMOUR XXVI

Cupid, dumbe-Idoll, peevish Saint of love,
No more shalt thou nor Saint nor Idoll be;
No God art thou, a Goddesse shee doth prove,
Of all thine honour shee hath robbed thee.
Thy Bowe, halfe broke, is peec'd with old desire;
Her Bowe is beauty with ten thousand strings
Of purest gold, tempred with vertues fire,
The least able to kyll an hoste of Kings.
Thy shafts be spent, and shee (to warre appointed)
Hydes in those christall quivers of her eyes
More Arrowes, with hart-piercing mettel poynted,
Then there be starres at midnight in the skyes.
With these she steales mens harts for her reliefe,
Yet happy he thats robd of such a thiefe!

AMOUR XXVII

My Love makes hote the fire whose heat is spent,
The water moisture from my teares deriveth,
And my strong sighes the ayres weake force reviveth:
Thus love, tears, sighes, maintaine each one his element.
The fire, vnto my love, compare a painted fire,
The water, to my teares as drops to Oceans be,
The ayre, vnto my sighes as Eagle to the flie,
The passions of dispaire but joyes to my desire.
Onely my love is in the fire ingraved,

Onely my teares by Oceans may be gessed,
Onely my sighes are by the ayre expressed;
Yet fire, water, ayre, of nature not deprived.
Whilst fire, water, ayre, twixt heaven and earth shal be,
My love, my teares, my sighes, extinguisht cannot be.

AMOUR XXVIII

Some wits there be which lyke my method well,
And say my verse runnes in a lofty vayne;
Some say, I have a passing pleasing straine,
Some say that in my humour I excell.
Some who reach not the height of my conceite,
They say, (as Poets doe) I vse to fayne,
And in bare words paynt out my passions payne:
Thus sundry men their sundry minds repeate.
I passe not I how men affected be,
Nor who commend, or discommend my verse;
It pleaseth me if I my plaints rehearse,
And in my lynes if shee my love may see.
I prove my verse autentique still in thys,
Who writes my Mistres praise can never write amisse.

AMOUR XXIX

O eyes! behold your happy Hesperus,
That luckie Load-starre of eternall light,
Left as that sunne alone to comfort vs,
When our worlds sunne is vanisht out of sight.
O starre of starres! fayre Planet mildly mooving,
O Lampe of vertue! sun-bright, ever shyning,
O mine eyes Comet! so admyr'd by loving,
O cleerest day-starre! never more declyning.
O our worlds wonder! crowne of heaven above,
Thrice happy be those eyes which may behold thee!
Lov'd more then life, yet onely art his love
Whose glorious hand immortal hath enrold thee!
O blessed fayre! now vaile those heavenly eyes,
That I may blesse mee at thy sweet arise.

AMOUR XXX

Three sorts of serpents doe resemble thee;
That daungerous eye-killing Cockatrice,
Th' inchaunting Syren, which doth so entice,

The weeping Crocodile; these vile pernicious three.
The Basiliske his nature takes from thee,
Who for my life in secret wait do'st lye,
And to my heart send'st poyson from thine eye:
Thus do I feele the paine, the cause yet cannot see.
Faire-mayd no more, but Mayr-maid be thy name,
Who with thy sweet aluring harmony
Hast playd the thiefe, and stolne my hart from me,
And, like a Tyrant, mak'st my griefe thy game.
The Crocodile, who, when thou hast me slaine,
Lament'st my death with teares of thy disdaine.

AMOUR XXXI

Sitting alone, love bids me goe and write;
Reason plucks backe, commaunding me to stay,
Boasting that shee doth still direct the way,
Els senceles love could never once indite.
Love, growing angry, vexed at the spleene,
And scorning Reasons maymed Argument,
Straight taxeth Reason, wanting to invent
Where shee with Love conversing hath not beene.
Reason, reproched with this coy disdaine,
Dispighteth Love, and laugheth at her folly,
And Love, contemning Reasons reason wholy,
Thought her in weight too light by many a graine.
Reason, put back, doth out of sight remove,
And Love alone finds reason in my love.

AMOUR XXXII

Those teares, which quench my hope, still kindle my desire,
Those sighes, which coole my hart, are coles vnto my love,
Disdayne, Ice to my life, is to my soule a fire:
With teares, sighes, and disdaine, this contrary I prove.
Quenchles desire makes hope burne, dryes my teares,
Love heats my hart, my hart-heat my sighes warmeth;
With my soules fire my life disdaine out-weares,
Desire, my love, my soule, my hope, hart, and life charmeth.
My hope becomes a friend to my desire,
My hart imbraceth Love, Love doth imbrace my hart;
My life a Phoenix is in my soules fire,
From thence (they vow) they never will depart.
Desire, my love, my soule, my hope, my hart, my life,
With teares, sighes, and disdaine, shall have immortal strife.

AMOUR XXXIII

Whilst thus mine eyes doe surfet with delight,
My wofull hart, imprisond in my breast,
Wishing to be trans-formd into my sight,
To looke on her by whom mine eyes are blest;
But whilst mine eyes thus greedily doe gaze,
Behold! their obiects over-soone depart,
And treading in this never-ending maze,
Wish now to be trans-formd into my hart:
My hart, surcharg'd with thoughts, sighes in abundance raise,
My eyes, made dim with lookes, poure down a flood of tears;
And whilst my hart and eye envy each others praise,
My dying lookes and thoughts are peiz'd in equall feares:
And thus, whilst sighes and teares together doe contende,
Each one of these doth ayde vnto the other lende.

AMOUR XXXIV

My fayre, looke from those turrets of thine eyes,
Into the Ocean of a troubled minde,
Where my poor soule, the Barke of sorrow, lyes,
Left to the mercy of the waves and winde.
See where she flotes, laden with purest love,
Which those fayre Ilands of thy lookes affoord,
Desiring yet a thousand deaths to prove,
Then so to cast her Ballase overboard.
See how her sayles be rent, her tacklings worne,
Her Cable broke, her surest Anchor lost:
Her Marryners doe leave her all forlorne,
Yet how shee bends towards that blessed Coast!
Loe! where she drownes in stormes of thy displeasure,
Whose worthy prize should have enricht thy treasure.

AMOUR XXXV

See, chaste Diana, where my harmles hart,
Rouz'd from my breast, his sure and safest layre,
Nor chaste by hound, nor forc'd by Hunters arte,
Yet see how right he comes vnto my fayre.
See how my Deere comes to thy Beauties stand,
And there stands gazing on those darting eyes,
Whilst from theyr rayes, by Cupids skilfull hand,
Into his hart the piercing Arrow flyes.
See how he lookes upon his bleeding wound,

Whilst thus he panteth for his latest breath,
And, looking on thee, falls upon the ground,
Smyling, as though he gloried in his death.
And wallowing in his blood, some lyfe yet laft;
His stone-cold lips doth kisse the blessed shaft.

AMOUR XXXVI

Sweete, sleepe so arm'd with Beauties arrowes darting,
Sleepe in thy Beauty, Beauty in sleepe appeareth;
Sleepe lightning Beauty, Beauty sleepes, darknes cleereth,
Sleepes wonder Beauty, wonders to worlds imparting.
Sleep watching Beauty, Beauty waking, sleepe guarding
Beauty in sleepe, sleepe in Beauty charmed,
Sleepes aged coldnes with Beauties fire warmed,
Sleepe with delight, Beauty with love rewarding.
Sleepe and Beauty, with equall forces stryuing,
Beauty her strength vnto sleepes weaknes lending,
Sleepe with Beauty, Beauty with sleepe contending,
Yet others force the others force reviving,
And others foe the others foe imbrace.
Myne eyes beheld thys conflict in thy face.

AMOUR XXXVII

I ever love where never hope appeares,
Yet hope drawes on my never-hoping care,
And my lives hope would die but for dyspaire;
My never certaine joy breeds ever-certaine feares.
Vncertaine dread gyues wings vnto my hope,
Yet my hopes wings are loden so with feare,
As they cannot ascend to my hopes spheare,
Yet feare gyues them more then a heavenly scope.
Yet this large roome is bounded with dyspaire,
So my love is still fettered with vaine hope,
And lyberty deprives him of hys scope,
And thus am I imprisond in the ayre:
Then, sweet Dispaire, awhile hold up thy head,
Or all my hope for sorrow will be dead.

AMOUR XXXVIII

If chaste and pure devotion of my youth,
Or glorie of my Aprill-springing yeeres,
Vnfained love in naked simple truth,

A thousand vowes, a thousand sighes and teares;
Or if a world of faithful service done,
Words, thoughts, and deeds devoted to her honor,
Or eyes that have beheld her as theyr sunne,
With admiration ever looking on her:
A lyfe that never joyd but in her love,
A soule that ever hath ador'd her name,
A fayth that time nor fortune could not move,
A Muse that vnto heaven hath raised her fame.
Though these, nor these deserve to be imbraced,
Yet, faire vnkinde, too good to be disgraced.

AMOUR XXXIX

Die, die, my soule, and never taste of joy,
If sighes, nor teares, nor vowes, nor prayers can move;
If fayth and zeale be but esteemd a toy,
And kindnes be vnkindnes in my love.
Then, with vnkindnes, Love, revenge thy wrong:
O sweet'st revenge that ere the heavens gave!
And with the swan record thy dying song,
And praise her still to thy vntimely grave.
So in loves death shall loves perfection prove
That love divine which I have borne to you,
By doome concealed to the heavens above,
That yet the world vnworthy never knew;
Whose pure Idea never tongue exprest:
I feele, you know, the heavens can tell the rest.

AMOUR XL

O thou unkindest fayre! most fayrest shee,
In thine eyes tryumph murthering my poore hart,
Now doe I sweare by heavens, before we part,
My halfe-slaine hart shall take revenge on thee.
Thy mother dyd her lyfe to death resigne,
And thou an Angell art, and from above;
Thy father was a man, that will I prove,
Yet thou a Goddesse art, and so divine.
And thus, if thou be not of humaine kinde,
A Bastard on both sides needes must thou be;
Our Lawes allow no land to basterdy:
By natures Lawes we thee a bastard finde.
Then hence to heaven, vnkind, for thy childs part:
Goe bastard goe, for sure of thence thou art.

Rare of-spring of my thoughts, my dearest Love,
Begot by fancy on sweet hope exhortiue,
In whom all purenes with perfection strove,
Hurt in the Embryon makes my joyes abhortive.
And you, my sighes, Symtomas of my woe,
The dolefull Anthems of my endelesse care,
Lyke idle Ecchoes ever answering; so,
The mournfull accents of my loves dispayre.
And thou, Conceite, the shadow of my blisse,
Declyning with the setting of my sunne,
Springing with that, and fading straight with this,
Now hast thou end, and now thou wast begun:
Now was thy pryme, and loe! is now thy waine;
Now wast thou borne, now in thy cradle slayne.

Plac'd in the forlorne hope of all dispayre
Against the Forte where Beauties Army lies,
Assayld with death, yet armed with gastly feare,
Loe! thus my love, my lyfe, my fortune tryes.
Wounded with Arrowes from thy lightning eyes,
My tongue in payne my harts counsels bewraying,
My rebell thought for me in Ambushe lyes,
To my lyves foe her Chieftaine still betraying.
Record my love in Ocean waves (unkind)
Cast my desarts into the open ayre,
Commit my words vnto the fleeting wind,
Cancell my name, and blot it with dispayre;
So shall I bee as I had never beene,
Nor my disgraces to the world be seene.

Why doe I speake of joy, or write of love,
When my hart is the very Den of horror,
And in my soule the paynes of hell I prove,
With all his torments and infernall terror?
Myne eyes want teares thus to bewayle my woe,
My brayne is dry with weeping all too long;
My sighes be spent with griefe and sighing so,
And I want words for to expresse my wrong.
But still, distracted in loves lunacy,

And Bedlam like thus raving in my griefe,
Now rayle upon her hayre, now on her eye,
Now call her Goddesse, then I call her thiefe;
Now I deny her, then I doe confesse her,
Now I doe curse her, then againe I blesse her.

AMOUR XLIV

My hart the Anvile where my thoughts doe beate,
My words the hammers fashioning my desire,
My breast the forge, including all the heate,
Love is the fuell which maintaines the fire:
My sighes the bellowes which the flame increaseth,
Filling mine eares with noise and nightly groning,
Toyling with paine my labour never ceaseth,
In greevous passions my woes styll bemoning.
Myne eyes with teares against the fire stryving,
With scorching gleed my hart to cynders turneth;
But with those drops the coles againe revyving,
Still more and more vnto my torment burneth.
With Sisiphus thus doe I role the stone,
And turne the wheele with damned Ixion.

AMOUR XLV

Blacke pytchy Night, companyon of my woe,
The Inne of care, the Nurse of drery sorrow,
Why lengthnest thou thy darkest howres so,
Still to prolong my long tyme lookt-for morrow?
Thou Sable shadow, Image of dispayre,
Portraite of hell, the ayres black mourning weed,
Recorder of revenge, remembrancer of care,
The shadow and the vaile of every sinfull deed.
Death like to thee, so lyve thou still in death,
The grave of joy, prison of dayes delight.
Let heavens withdraw their sweet Ambrozian breath,
Nor Moone nor stars lend thee their shining light;
For thou alone renew'st that olde desire,
Which still torments me in dayes burning fire.

AMOUR XLVI

Sweete secrecie, what tongue can tell thy worth?
What mortall pen sufficiently can prayse thee?
What curious Pensill serves to lim thee forth?

What Muse hath power above thy height to raise thee?
Strong locke of kindnesse, Closet of loves store,
Harts Methridate, the soules preservative;
O vertue! which all vertues doe adore,
Cheefe good, from whom all good things wee derive.
O rare effect! true bond of friendships measure,
Conceite of Angels, which all wisdom teachest;
O, richest Casket of all heavenly treasure,
In secret silence which such wonders preachest.
O purest mirror! wherein men may see
The lively Image of Divinitie.

AMOUR XLVII

The golden Sunne upon his fiery wheeles
The horned Ram doth in his course awake,
And of just length our night and day doth make,
Flinging the Fishes backward with his heeles:
Then to the Tropicke takes his full Careere,
Trotting his sun-steeds till the Palfrays sweat,
Bayting the Lyon in his furious heat,
Till Virgins smyles doe sound his sweet reteere.
But my faire Planet, who directs me still,
Vnkindly such distemperature doth bring,
Makes Summer Winter, Autumne in the Spring,
Crossing sweet nature by unruly will.
Such is the sunne who guides my youthfull season,
Whose thwarting course deprives the world of reason.

AMOUR XLVIII

Who list to praise the dayes delicious lyght,
Let him compare it to her heavenly eye,
The sun-beames to the lustre of her sight;
So may the learned like the similie.
The mornings Crimson to her lyps alike,
The sweet of Eden to her breathes perfume,
The fayre Elizia to her fayrer cheeke,
Vnto her veynes the onely Phœnix plume.
The Angels tresses to her tressed hayre,
The Galixia to her more then white.
Praysing the fayrest, compare it to my faire,
Still naming her in naming all delight.
So may he grace all these in her alone,
Superlative in all comparison.

Define my love, and tell the joyes of heaven,
Expresse my woes, and shew the paynes of hell;
Declare what fate unlucky starres have given,
And aske a world upon my life to dwell.
Make knowne that fayth vnkindnes could not move;
Compare my worth with others base desert:
Let vertue be the tuch-stone of my love,
So may the heavens reade wonders in my hart.
Behold the Clowdes which have eclips'd my sunne,
And view the crosses which my course doth let;
Tell mee, if ever since the world begunne,
So faire a Morning had so foule a set?
And, by all meanes, let black vnkindnes prove
The patience of so rare, divine a love.

When I first ended, then I first began;
The more I travell, further from my rest;
Where most I lost, there most of all I wan;
Pyned with hunger, rysing from a feast.
Mee thinks I flee, yet want I legs to goe,
Wise in conceite, in acte a very sot;
Ravisht with joy amidst a hell of woe,
What most I seeme, that surest I am not.
I build my hopes a world above the skye,
Yet with a Mole I creepe into the earth:
In plenty am I starv'd with penury,
And yet I serfet in the greatest dearth.
I have, I want, dispayre, and yet desire,
Burn'd in a Sea of Ice, and drown'd amidst a fire.

Goe you, my lynes, Embassadours of love,
With my harts tribute to her conquering eyes,
From whence, if you one tear of pitty move
For all my woes, that onely shall suffise.
When you Minerva in the sunne behold,
At her perfections stand you then and gaze,
Where in the compasse of a Marygold,
Meridianis sits within a maze.
And let Invention of her beauty vaunt

When Dorus sings his sweet Pamelas love,
And tell the Gods, Mars is predominant,
Seated with Sol, and weares Minervas glove:
And tell the world, that in the world there is
A heaven on earth, on earth no heaven but this.

SONNETS FROM THE 1599 EDITION

SONNET I

The worlds faire Rose, and Henries frosty fire,
Iohns tyrannie; and chast Matilda's wrong,
Th'inraged Queene, and furious Mortimer,
The scourge of Fraunce, and his chast loue I song;
Deposed Richard, Isabell exil'd,
The gallant Tudor, and fayre Katherine,
Duke Humfrey, and old Cobhams haplesse child,
Couragious Pole, and that braue spiritfull Queene;
Edward, and that delicious London Dame,
Brandon, and that rich dowager of Fraunce,
Surrey, with his fayre paragon of fame,
Dudleys mishap, and vertuous Grays mischance;
Their seuerall loues since I before haue showne,
Now giue me leaue at last to sing mine owne.

SONNET III

Many there be excelling in this kind,
Whose well trick'd rimes with all inuention swell,
Let each commend as best shall like his minde,
Some Sidney, Constable, some Daniell.
That thus theyr names familiarly I sing,
Let none think them disparaged to be,
Poore men with reuerence may speake of a King,
And so may these be spoken of by mee;
My wanton verse nere keepes one certaine stay,
But now, at hand; then, seekes inuention far,
And with each little motion runnes astray,
Wilde, madding, iocond, and irreguler;
Like me that lust, my honest merry rimes,
Nor care for Criticke, nor regard the times.

SONNET IX

Love once would daunce within my Mistres eye,
And wanting musique fitting for the place,
Swore that I should the Instrument supply,
And sodainly presents me with her face:
Straightwayes my pulse playes liuely in my vaines,
My panting breath doth keepe a meaner time,
My quau'ring artiers be the Tenours Straynes,
My trembling sinewes serue the Counterchime,
My hollow sighs the deepest base doe beare,
True diapazon in distincted sound:
My panting hart the treble makes the ayre,
And descants finely on the musiques ground;
Thus like a Lute or Violl did I lye,
Whilst the proud slaue daunc'd galliards in her eye.

SONNET XI

To the Moone

Phæbe looke downe, and here behold in mee,
The elements within thy sphere inclosed,
How kindly Nature plac'd them vnder thee,
And in my world, see how they are disposed;
My hope is earth, the lowest, cold and dry,
The grosser mother of deepe melancholie,
Water my teares, coold with humidity,
Wan, flegmatick, inclind by nature wholie;
My sighs, the ayre, hote, moyst, ascending hier,
Subtile of sanguine, dy'de in my harts dolor,
My thoughts, they be the element of fire,
Hote, dry, and piercing, still inclind to choller,
Thine eye the Orbe vnto all these, from whence,
Proceeds th' effects of powerfull influence.

SONNET XXI

You cannot love my pretty hart, and why?
There was a time, you told me that you would,
But now againe you will the same deny,
If it might please you, would to God you could;
What will you hate? nay, that you will not neither,
Nor love, nor hate, how then? what will you do,
What will you keepe a meane then betwixt eyther?
Or will you love me, and yet hate me to?
Yet serves not this, what next, what other shift?

You will, and will not, what a coyle is heere,
I see your craft, now I perceaue your drift,
And all this while, I was mistaken there.
Your love and hate is this, I now doe prove you,
You love in hate, by hate to make me love you.

SONNET XXIII

To the Spheares

Thou which do'st guide this little world of loue,
Thy planets mansions heere thou mayst behold,
My brow the spheare where Saturne still doth moue,
Wrinkled with cares: and withered, dry, and cold;
Mine eyes the Orbe where Iupiter doth trace,
Which gently smile because they looke on thee,
Mars in my swarty visage takes his place,
Made leane with loue, where furious conflicts bee.
Sol in my breast with his hote scorching flame,
And in my hart alone doth Venus raigne:
Mercury my hands the Organs of thy fame,
And Luna glides in my fantastick braine;
The starry heauen thy prayse by me exprest,
Thou the first moouer, guiding all the rest.

SONNET XXVII

I gave my faith to Loue, Loue his to mee,
That hee and I, sworne brothers should remaine,
Thus fayth receiv'd, fayth given back againe,
Who would imagine bond more sure could be?
Loue flies to her, yet holds he my fayth taken,
Thus from my vertue raiseth my offence,
Making me guilty by mine innocence;
And surer bond by beeing so forsaken,
He makes her aske what I before had vow'd,
Giving her that, which he had given me,
I bound by him, and he by her made free,
Who ever so hard breach of fayth alow'd?
Speake you that should of right and wrong discusse,
Was right ere wrong'd, or wrong ere righted thus?

SONNET XXXIV

To Admiration

Maruaile not Loue, though I thy power admire,
Rauish'd a world beyond the farthest thought,
That knowing more then ever hath beene taught,
That I am onely starv'd in my desire;
Maruaile not Loue, though I thy power admire,
Ayming at things exceeding all perfection,
To wisedoms selfe, to minister direction,
That I am onely staru'd in my desire;
Maruaile not Loue, though I thy power admire,
Though my conceite I farther seeme to bend,
Then possibly invention can extend,
And yet am onely staru'd in my desire;
If thou wilt wonder, heers the wonder love,
That this to mee doth yet no wonder prove.

SONNET XLIII

Whilst thus my pen striues to eternize thee,
Age rules my lines with wrincles in my face,
Where in the Map of all my misery,
Is modeld out the world of my disgrace,
Whilst in despight of tyrannizing times,
Medea like I make thee young againe,
Proudly thou scorn'st my world-outwearing rimes,
And murther'st vertue with thy coy disdaine;
And though in youth, my youth untimely perrish,
To keepe thee from obliuion and the graue,
Ensuing ages yet my rimes shall cherrish,
Where I entomb'd, my better part shall saue;
And though this earthly body fade and die
My name shall mount upon eternitie.

SONNET XLIV

Muses which sadly sit about my chayre,
Drownd in the teares extorted by my lines,
With heauy sighs whilst thus I breake the ayre,
Paynting my passions in these sad dissignes,
Since she disdaines to blesse my happy verse,
The strong built Trophies to her liuing fame,
Ever hence-forth my bosome be your hearse,
Wherein the world shal now entombe her name,
Enclose my musick you poor sencelesse walls,
Sith she is deafe and will not heare my mones,
Soften your selves with every teare that falls,

Whilst I like Orpheus sing to trees and stones:
Which with my plaints seeme yet with pitty moved,
Kinder then she who I so long have loved.

SONNET XLV

Thou leaden braine, which censur'st what I write,
And say'st my lines be dull and doe not moue,
I meruaile not thou feelst not my delight,
Which never felt my fiery tuch of loue.
But thou whose pen hath like a Pack-horse serv'd,
Whose stomack unto gaule hath turn'd thy foode,
Whose sences like poore prisoners hunger-starv'd,
Whose griefe hath parch'd thy body, dry'd thy blood.
Thou which hast scorned life, and hated death,
And in a moment mad, sober, glad, and sorry,
Thou which hast band thy thoughts and curst thy breath,
With thousand plagues more then in purgatory.
Thou thus whose spirit Loue in his fire refines,
Come thou and reade, admire, applaud my lines.

SONNET LV

Truce gentle love, a parly now I crave,
Me thinks, 'tis long since first these wars begun,
Nor thou nor I, the better yet can have:
Bad is the match where neither party wone.
I offer free conditions of faire peace,
My hart for hostage, that it shall remaine,
Discharge our forces heere, let malice cease,
So for my pledge, thou give me pledge againe.
Or if nothing but death will serve thy turne,
Still thirsting for subversion of my state;
Doe what thou canst, raze, massacre, and burne,
Let the world see the utmost of thy hate:
I send defiance, since if overthrowne,
Thou vanquishing, the conquest is mine owne.

SONNET LVI

A Consonet

Eyes with your teares, blind if you bee,
Why have these teares such eyes to see,
Poore eyes, if yours teares cannot moue,

My teares, eyes, then must mone my love,
Then eyes, since you have lost your sight,
Weepe still, and teares shall lend you light,
Till both desolv'd, and both want might.
No, no, cleere eyes, you are not blind,
But in my teares discerne my mind:
Teares be the language which you speake,
Which my hart wanting, yet must breake;
My tongue must cease to tell my wrongs,
And make my sighs to get them tongs,
Yet more then this to her belongs.

SONNET LVII

To Lucie Countesse of Bedford

Great Lady, essence of my chiefest good,
Of the most pure and finest tempred spirit,
Adorn'd with gifts, enobled by thy blood,
Which by discent true vertue do'st inherit:
That vertue which no fortune can deprive,
Which thou by birth tak'st from thy gracious mother,
Whose royall minds with equall motion striue,
Which most in honour shall excell the other;
Vnto thy fame my Muse herself shall taske,
Which rain'st upon me thy sweet golden showers,
And but thy selfe, no subject will I aske,
Upon whose praise my soule shall spend her powers.
Sweet Lady yet, grace this poore Muse of mine,
Whose faith, whose zeale, whose life, whose all is thine.

SONNET LVIII

To the Lady Anne Harington

Madam, my words cannot expresse my mind,
My zealous kindnes to make knowne to you,
When your desarts all seuerally I find;
In this attempt of me doe claim their due,
Your gracious kindnes that doth claime my hart;
Your bounty bids my hand to make it knowne,
Of me your vertues each doe claime a part,
And leave me thus the least part of mine owne.
What should commend your modesty and wit,
Is by your wit and modesty commended
And standeth dumbe, in much admiring it,

And where it should begin, it there is ended;
Returning this your prayses onely due,
And to your selfe say you are onely you.

SONNETS FROM THE 1602 EDITION

SONNET XII

To Lunacie

As other men, so I my selfe doe muse,
Why in this sort I wrest Inuention so,
And why these giddy metaphors I vse,
Leaving the path the greater part doe goe;
I will resolve you; I am lunaticke,
And ever this in mad men you shall finde,
What they last thought on when the braine grew sick,
In most distraction keepe that still in minde.
Thus talking idely in this bedlam fit,
Reason and I, (you must conceiue) are twaine,
'Tis nine yeeres, now, since first I lost my wit
Beare with me, then, though troubled be my braine;
With diet and correction, men distraught,
(Not too farre past) may to their wits be brought.

SONNET XVII

If hee from heaven that filch'd that liuing fire,
Condemn'd by love to endlesse torment be,
I greatly meruaile how you still goe free,
That farre beyond Promethius did aspire?
The fire he stole, although of heauenly kinde,
Which from above he craftily did take,
Of liveles clods vs living men to make,
Againe bestow'd in temper of the mind.
But you broke in to heauens immortall store,
Where vertue, honour, wit, and beautie lay,
Which taking thence, you have escap'd away,
Yet stand as free as ere you did before.
But old Promethius punish'd for his rape,
Thus poore theeues suffer, when the greater scape.

SONNET XXV

To Folly

With fooles and children good discretion beares,
Then honest people beare with Loue and me,
Nor older yet, nor wiser made by yeeres,
Amongst the rest of fooles and children be;
Loves still a Baby, playes with gaudes and toyes,
And like a wanton sports with every feather,
And Idiots still are running after boyes,
Then fooles and children fitt'st to goe together;
He still as young as when he first was borne,
No wiser I, then when as young as he,
You that behold vs, laugh vs not to scorne,
Give Nature thanks, you are not such as we;
Yet fooles and children sometimes tell in play,
Some wise in showe, more fooles in deede, then they.

SONNET XXVII

I heare some say, this man is not in love,
Who, can he love? a likely thing they say:
Reade but his verse, and it will easily prove;
O judge not rashly (gentle Sir) I pray,
Because I loosely tryfle in this sort,
As one that faine his sorrowes would beguile:
You now suppose me, all this time in sport,
And please your selfe with this conceit the while.
You shallow censures; sometime see you not
In greatest perills some men pleasant be,
Where fame by death is onely to be got,
They resolute, so stands the case with me;
Where other men, in depth of passion cry,
I laugh at fortune, as in jest to die.

SONNET XXXI

To such as say thy love I over-prize,
And doe not sticke to terme my praises folly,
Against these folkes that think them selves so wise,
I thus appose my force of reason wholly,
Though I give more, then well affords my state,
In which expense the most suppose me vaine,
Would yeeld them nothing at the easiest rate,
Yet at this price, returnes me treble gaine,
They value not, unskilfull how to vse,

And I give much, because I gaine thereby,
I that thus take, or they that thus refuse,
Whether are these deccaued then, or I?
In every thing I hold this maxim still,
The circumstance doth make it good or ill.

SONNET XLI

Deare, why should you commaund me to my rest
When now the night doth summon all to sleepe?
Me thinks this time becommeth louers best,
Night was ordained together friends to keepe.
How happy are all other living things,
Which though the day disjoyne by severall flight,
The quiet evening yet together brings,
And each returnes unto his love at night.
O thou that art so curteous vnto all,
Why shouldst thou Night abuse me onely thus,
That every creature to his kinde doost call,
And yet tis thou doost onely sever us.
Well could I wish it would be ever day,
If when night comes you bid me goe away.

SONNET LXIII

To the High and Mighty Prince, James, King of Scots

Not thy grave Counsells, nor thy Subiects loue,
Nor all that famous Scottish royaltie,
Or what thy soveraigne greatnes may approue,
Others in vaine doe but historifie,
When thine owne glorie from thy selfe doth spring,
As though thou did'st, all meaner prayses scorne:
Of Kings a Poet, and the Poets King,
They Princes, but thou Prophets do'st adorne;
Whilst others by their Empires are renown'd,
Thou do'st enrich thy Scotland with renowne,
And Kings can but with Diadems be crown'd,
But with thy Laurell, thou doo'st crowne thy Crowne;
That they whose pens, euen life to Kings doe giue,
In thee a King, shall seeke them selves to live.

SONNET LXVI

To the Lady L.S.

Bright starre of Beauty, on whose eyelids sit,
A thousand Nimph-like and enamoured Graces,
The Goddesses of memory and wit,
Which in due order take their severall places,
In whose deare bosome, sweet delicious love,
Layes downe his quiver, that he once did beare,
Since he that blessed Paradice did prove,
Forsooke his mothers lap to sport him there.
Let others strive to entertaine with words,
My soule is of another temper made;
I hold it vile that vulgar wit affords,
Devouring time my faith, shall not invade:
Still let my praise be honoured thus by you,
Be you most worthy, whilst I be most true.

SONNETS FROM THE 1605 EDITION

SONNET XLIII

Why should your faire eyes with such soveraine grace,
Dispearse their raies on every vulgar spirit,
Whilst I in darknes in the selfesame place,
Get not one glance to recompence my merit:
So doth the plow-man gaze the wandring starre,
And onely rests contented with the light,
That never learnd what constellations are,
Beyond the bent of his vnknowing sight.
O why should beautie (custome to obey)
To their grosse sence applie her selfe so ill?
Would God I were as ignorant as they
When I am made unhappy by my skill;
Onely compeld on this poore good to boast,
Heauens are not kind to them that know them most.

SONNET XLVI

Plain-path'd Experience the unlearneds guide,
Her simple followers evidently shewes,
Sometime what schoolemen scarcely can decide,
Nor yet wise Reason absolutely knowes:
In making triall of a murther wrought,
If the vile actor of the heinous deede,
Neere the dead bodie happily be brought,

Oft hath been prov'd the breathlesse coarse will bleed;
She comming neere that my poore hart hath slaine,
Long since departed, (to the world no more)
The auncient wounds no longer can containe,
But fall to bleeding as they did before:
But what of this? should she to death be led,
It furthers justice, but helpes not the dead.

SONNET XLVII

In pride of wit, when high desire of fame
Gave life and courage to my labouring pen,
And first the sound and vertue of my name,
Won grace and credit in the eares of men:
With those the thronged Theaters that presse,
I in the circuite for the Lawrell strove,
Where the full praise I freely must confesse,
In heate of blood a modest minde might moue:
With showts and daps at everie little pawse,
When the prowd round on everie side hath rung,
Sadly I sit unmou'd with the applawse,
As though to me it nothing did belong:
No publique glorie vainely I pursue,
The praise I striue, is to eternize you.

SONNET L

As in some Countries far remote from hence,
The wretched creature destined to die,
Having the judgement due to his offence,
By Surgeons begg'd, their Art on him to trie:
Which on the living worke without remorce,
First make incision on each maistring vaine,
Then stanch the bleeding, then transperce the coarse,
And with their balmes recure the wounds againe,
Then poison and with Phisicke him restore,
Not that they feare the hopelesse man to kill,
But their experience to encrease the more;
Even so my Mistresse works upon my ill,
By curing me, and killing me each howre,
Onely to shew her beauties soveraigne powre.

SONNET LI

Calling to minde since first my love begunne,

Th' incertaine times oft varying in their course,
How things still vnexpectedly have runne,
As please the fates, by their resistlesse force:
Lastly, mine eyes amazedly have scene,
Essex great fall, Tyrone his peace to gaine,
The quiet end of that long-living Queene,
This Kings faire entrance, and our peace with Spaine,
We and the Dutch at length our selves to sever.
Thus the world doth, and evermore shall reele,
Yet to my goddesse am I constant ever;
How ere blind fortune turne her giddy wheele:
Though heaven and earth prove both to mee untrue,
Yet am I still inuiolate to you.

SONNET LVII

You best discern'd of my interior eies,
And yet your graces outwardly divine,
Whose deare remembrance in my bosome lies,
Too riche a relique for so poore a shrine:
You in whome Nature chose herselfe to view,
When she her owne perfection would admire,
Bestowing all her excellence on you;
At whose pure eies Love lights his halowed fire,
Even as a man that in some traunce hath scene,
More than his wondring uttrance can vnfolde,
That rapt in spirite in better worlds hath beene,
So must your praise distractedly be tolde;
Most of all short, when I should shew you most,
In your perfections altogether lost.

SONNET LVIII

In former times, such as had store of coyne,
In warres at home, or when for conquests bound,
For feare that some their treasures should purloyne,
Gave it to keepe to spirites within the ground;
And to attend it, them so strongly tide,
Till they return'd, home when they never came,
Such as by art to get the same have tride,
From the strong spirits by no means get the same,
Neerer you come, that further flies away,
Striuing to holde it strongly in the deepe:
Even as this spirit, so she alone doth play,
With those rich Beauties heauen gives her to keepe:
Pitty so left, to coldenes of her blood,

Not to availe her, nor do others good.

To Sir Walter Aston, Knight of the Honourable Order of the Bath, and My Most Worthy Patron

I will not striue m' inuention to inforce,
With needlesse words your eyes to entertaine,
T' obserue the formall ordinarie course
That euerie one so vulgarly doth faine:
Our interchanged and deliberate choise,
Is with more firme and true election sorted,
Then stands in censure of the common voice.
That with light humor fondly is transported:
Nor take I patterne of another's praise,
Then what my pen may constantly avow.
Nor walke more publique nor obscurer waies
Then vertue bids, and iudgement will allow;
So shall my tone, and best endeuours serue you,
And still shall studie, still so to deserue you.
Michael Drayton.

IDEA

An Elizabethan Sonnet Cycle

TO THE READER OF THESE SONNETS

Into these loves who but for passion looks,
At this first sight here let him lay them by,
And seek elsewhere in turning other books,
Which better may his labour satisfy.
No far-fetched sigh shall ever wound my breast;
Love from mine eye a tear shall never wring;
Nor in "Ah me's!" my whining sonnets drest,
A libertine fantasticly I sing.
My verse is the true image of my mind,
Ever in motion, still desiring change;
To choice of all variety inclined,
And in all humours sportively I range.
My muse is rightly of the English strain,
That cannot long one fashion entertain.

IDEA I

Like an adventurous sea-farer am I,
Who hath some long and dang'rous voyage been,
And called to tell of his discovery,
How far he sailed, what countries he had seen,
Proceeding from the port whence he put forth,
Shows by his compass how his course he steered,
When east, when west, when south, and when by north,
As how the pole to every place was reared,
What capes he doubled, of what continent,
The gulfs and straits that strangely he had past,
Where most becalmed, where with foul weather spent,
And on what rocks in peril to be cast:
Thus in my love, time calls me to relate
My tedious travels and oft-varying fate.

IDEA II

My heart was slain, and none but you and I;
Who should I think the murder should commit?
Since but yourself there was no creature by
But only I, guiltless of murdering it.
It slew itself; the verdict on the view
Do quit the dead, and me not accessary.
Well, well, I fear it will be proved by you,
The evidence so great a proof doth carry.
But O see, see, we need inquire no further!
Upon your lips the scarlet drops are found,
And in your eye the boy that did the murder,
Your cheeks yet pale since first he gave the wound!
By this I see, however things be past,
Yet heaven will still have murder out at last.

IDEA III

Taking my pen, with words to cast my woe,
Duly to count the sum of all my cares,
I find my griefs innumerable grow,
The reck'nings rise to millions of despairs.
And thus dividing of my fatal hours,
The payments of my love I read and cross;
Subtracting, set my sweets unto my sours,
My joys' arrearage leads me to my loss.
And thus mine eyes a debtor to thine eye,
Which by extortion gaineth all their looks,
My heart hath paid such grievous usury,
That all their wealth lies in thy beauty's books.

And all is thine which hath been due to me,
And I a bankrupt, quite undone by thee.

IDEA IV

Bright star of beauty, on whose eyelids sit
A thousand nymph-like and enamoured graces,
The goddesses of memory and wit,
Which there in order take their several places;
In whose dear bosom, sweet delicious love
Lays down his quiver which he once did bear,
Since he that blessèd paradise did prove,
And leaves his mother's lap to sport him there
Let others strive to entertain with words
My soul is of a braver mettle made;
I hold that vile which vulgar wit affords;
In me's that faith which time cannot invade.
Let what I praise be still made good by you;
Be you most worthy whilst I am most true!

IDEA V

Nothing but "No!" and "I!" and "I!" and "No!"
"How falls it out so strangely?" you reply.
I tell ye, Fair, I'll not be answered so,
With this affirming "No!" denying "I!"
I say "I love!" You slightly answer "I!"
I say "You love!" You pule me out a "No!"
I say "I die!" You echo me with "I!"
"Save me!" I cry; you sigh me out a "No!"
Must woe and I have naught but "No!" and "I!"?
No "I!" am I, if I no more can have.
Answer no more; with silence make reply,
And let me take myself what I do crave;
Let "No!" and "I!" with I and you be so,
Then answer "No!" and "I!" and "I!" and "No!"

[Footnote A: The "I" of course equals "aye."]

IDEA VI

How many paltry, foolish, painted things,
That now in coaches trouble every street,
Shall be forgotten, whom no poet sings,
Ere they be well wrapped in their winding sheet!

Where I to thee eternity shall give,
When nothing else remaineth of these days,
And queens hereafter shall be glad to live
Upon the alms of thy superfluous praise;
Virgins and matrons reading these my rhymes,
Shall be so much delighted with thy story,
That they shall grieve they lived not in these times,
To have seen thee, their sex's only glory.
So shalt thou fly above the vulgar throng,
Still to survive in my immortal song.

IDEA VII

Love, in a humour, played the prodigal,
And bade my senses to a solemn feast;
Yet more to grace the company withal,
Invites my heart to be the chiefest guest.
No other drink would serve this glutton's turn,
But precious tears distilling from mine eyne,
Which with my sighs this epicure doth burn,
Quaffing carouses in this costly wine;
Where, in his cups, o'ercome with foul excess,
Straightways he plays a swaggering ruffian's part,
And at the banquet in his drunkenness,
Slew his dear friend, my kind and truest heart.
A gentle warning, friends, thus may you see,
What 'tis to keep a drunkard company!

IDEA VIII

There's nothing grieves me but that age should haste,
That in my days I may not see thee old;
That where those two clear sparkling eyes are placed,
Only two loopholes that I might behold;
That lovely archèd ivory-polished brow
Defaced with wrinkles, that I might but see;
Thy dainty hair, so curled and crispèd now,
Like grizzled moss upon some agèd tree;
Thy cheek now flush with roses, sunk and lean;
Thy lips, with age as any wafer thin!
Thy pearly teeth out of thy head so clean,
That when thou feed'st thy nose shall touch thy chin!
These lines that now thou scornst, which should delight thee,
Then would I make thee read but to despite thee.

IDEA IX

As other men, so I myself do muse
Why in this sort I wrest invention so,
And why these giddy metaphors I use,
Leaving the path the greater part do go.
I will resolve you. I'm a lunatic;
And ever this in madmen you shall find,
What they last thought of when the brain grew sick,
In most distraction they keep that in mind.
Thus talking idly in this bedlam fit,
Reason and I, you must conceive, are twain;
'Tis nine years now since first I lost my wit.
Bear with me then though troubled be my brain.
With diet and correction men distraught,
Not too far past, may to their wits be brought.

IDEA X

To nothing fitter can I thee compare
Than to the son of some rich penny-father,
Who having now brought on his end with care,
Leaves to his son all he had heaped together.
This new rich novice, lavish of his chest,
To one man gives, doth on another spend;
Then here he riots; yet amongst the rest,
Haps to lend some to one true honest friend.
Thy gifts thou in obscurity dost waste:
False friends, thy kindness born but to deceive thee;
Thy love that is on the unworthy placed;
Time hath thy beauty which with age will leave thee.
Only that little which to me was lent,
I give thee back when all the rest is spent.

IDEA XI

You're not alone when you are still alone;
O God! from you that I could private be!
Since you one were, I never since was one;
Since you in me, myself since out of me.
Transported from myself into your being,
Though either distant, present yet to either;
Senseless with too much joy, each other seeing;
And only absent when we are together.
Give me my self, and take your self again!
Devise some means but how I may forsake you!

So much is mine that doth with you remain,
That taking what is mine, with me I take you.
You do bewitch me! O that I could fly
From my self you, or from your own self I!

IDEA XII - TO THE SOUL

That learned Father which so firmly proves
The soul of man immortal and divine,
And doth the several offices define
Anima. - Gives her that name, as she the body moves.
Amor. - Then is she love, embracing charity.
Animus. - Moving a will in us, it is the mind;
Mens. - Retaining knowledge, still the same in kind.
Memoria. - As intellectual, it is memory.
Ratio. - In judging, reason only is her name.
Sensus. - In speedy apprehension, it is sense.
Conscientia. - In right and wrong they call her conscience;
Spiritus. - The spirit, when it to God-ward doth inflame:
These of the soul the several functions be,
Which my heart lightened by thy love doth see.

IDEA XIII - TO THE SHADOW

Letters and lines we see are soon defaced
Metals do waste and fret with canker's rust,
The diamond shall once consume to dust,
And freshest colours with foul stains disgraced;
Paper and ink can paint but naked words,
To write with blood of force offends the sight;
And if with tears, I find them all too light,
And sighs and signs a silly hope affords.
O sweetest shadow, how thou serv'st my turn!
Which still shalt be as long as there is sun,
Nor whilst the world is never shall be done;
Whilst moon shall shine or any fire shall burn,
That everything whence shadow doth proceed,
May in his shadow my love's story read.

IDEA XIV

If he, from heaven that filched that living fire,
Condemned by Jove to endless torment be,
I greatly marvel how you still go free
That far beyond Prometheus did aspire.

The fire he stole, although of heavenly kind,
Which from above he craftily did take,
Of lifeless clods us living men to make
He did bestow in temper of the mind.
But you broke into heaven's immortal store,
Where virtue, honour, wit, and beauty lay;
Which taking thence, you have escaped away,
Yet stand as free as e'er you did before.
Yet old Prometheus punished for his rape;
Thus poor thieves suffer when the greater 'scape.

IDEA XV - HIS REMEDY FOR LOVE

Since to obtain thee nothing me will stead,
I have a med'cine that shall cure my love.
The powder of her heart dried, when she's dead,
That gold nor honour ne'er had power to move;
Mixed with her tears that ne'er her true love crost,
Nor at fifteen ne'er longed to be a bride;
Boiled with her sighs, in giving up the ghost,
That for her late deceasèd husband died;
Into the same then let a woman breathe,
That being chid did never word reply;
With one thrice married's prayers, that did bequeath
A legacy to stale virginity.
If this receipt have not the power to win me,
Little I'll say, but think the devil's in me!

IDEA XVI - AN ALLUSION TO THE PHOENIX

'Mongst all the creatures in this spacious round
Of the birds' kind, the phoenix is alone,
Which best by you of living things is known;
None like to that, none like to you is found!
Your beauty is the hot and splend'rous sun;
The precious spices be your chaste desire,
Which being kindled by that heavenly fire,
Your life, so like the phoenix's begun.
Yourself thus burnèd in that sacred flame,
With so rare sweetness all the heavens perfuming;
Again increasing as you are consuming,
Only by dying born the very same.
And winged by fame you to the stars ascend;
So you of time shall live beyond the end.

IDEA XVII - TO TIME

Stay, speedy time! Behold, before thou pass
From age to age, what thou hast sought to see,
One in whom all the excellencies be,
In whom heaven looks itself as in a glass.
Time, look thou too in this translucent glass,
And thy youth past in this pure mirror see!
As the world's beauty in his infancy,
What it was then, and thou before it was.
Pass on and to posterity tell this--
Yet see thou tell but truly what hath been.
Say to our nephews that thou once hast seen
In perfect human shape all heavenly bliss;
And bid them mourn, nay more, despair with thee,
That she is gone, her like again to see.

IDEA XVIII - TO THE CELESTIAL NUMBERS

To this our world, to learning, and to heaven,
Three nines there are, to every one a nine;
One number of the earth, the other both divine;
One woman now makes three odd numbers even.
Nine orders first of angels be in heaven;
Nine muses do with learning still frequent:
These with the gods are ever resident.
Nine worthy women to the world were given.
My worthy one to these nine worthies addeth;
And my fair Muse, one Muse unto the nine.
And my good angel, in my soul divine!--
With one more order these nine orders gladdeth.
My Muse, my worthy, and my angel then
Makes every one of these three nines a ten.

IDEA XIX - TO HUMOUR

You cannot love, my pretty heart, and why?
There was a time you told me that you would,
But how again you will the same deny.
If it might please you, would to God you could!
What, will you hate? Nay, that you will not neither;
Nor love, nor hate! How then? What will you do?
What, will you keep a mean then betwixt either?
Or will you love me, and yet hate me too?
Yet serves not this! What next, what other shift?
You will, and will not; what a coil is here!

I see your craft, now I perceive your drift,
And all this while I was mistaken there.
Your love and hate is this, I now do prove you:
You love in hate, by hate to make me love you.

IDEA XX

An evil spirit, your beauty, haunts me still,
Wherewith, alas, I have been long possessed!
Which ceaseth not to tempt me to each ill,
Nor give me once but one poor minute's rest.
In me it speaks whether I sleep or wake;
And when by means to drive it out I try,
With greater torments then it me doth take,
And tortures me in most extremity.
Before my face it lays down my despairs,
And hastes me on unto a sudden death;
Now tempting me to drown myself in tears,
And then in sighing to give up my breath.
Thus am I still provoked to every evil,
By this good wicked spirit, sweet angel-devil.

IDEA XXI

A witless gallant a young wench that wooed--
Yet his dull spirit her not one jot could move--
Intreated me as e'er I wished his good,
To write him but one sonnet to his love.
When I as fast as e'er my pen could trot,
Poured out what first from quick invention came,
Nor never stood one word thereof to blot;
Much like his wit that was to use the same.
But with my verses he his mistress won,
Who doated on the dolt beyond all measure.
But see, for you to heaven for phrase I run,
And ransack all Apollo's golden treasure!
Yet by my troth, this fool his love obtains,
And I lose you for all my wit and pains!

IDEA XXII - TO FOLLY

With fools and children good discretion bears;
Then, honest people, bear with love and me,
Nor older yet nor wiser made by years,
Amongst the rest of fools and children be.

Love, still a baby, plays with gauds and toys,
And like a wanton sports with every feather,
And idiots still are running after boys;
Then fools and children fitt'st to go together.
He still as young as when he first was born,
Nor wiser I than when as young as he;
You that behold us, laugh us not to scorn;
Give nature thanks you are not such as we!
Yet fools and children sometimes tell in play;
Some wise in show, more fools indeed than they.

IDEA XXIII

Love, banished heaven, in earth was held in scorn,
Wand'ring abroad in need and beggary;
And wanting friends, though of a goddess born,
Yet craved the alms of such as passèd by.
I, like a man devout and charitable,
Clothèd the naked, lodged this wandering guest;
With sighs and tears still furnishing his table
With what might make the miserable blest.
But this ungrateful for my good desert,
Enticed my thoughts against me to conspire,
Who gave consent to steal away my heart,
And set my breast, his lodging, on a fire.
Well, well, my friends, when beggars grow thus bold,
No marvel then though charity grow cold.

IDEA XXIV

I hear some say, "This man is not in love!"
"Who! can he love? a likely thing!" they say.
"Read but his verse, and it will easily prove!"
O, judge not rashly, gentle Sir, I pray!
Because I loosely trifle in this sort,
As one that fain his sorrows would beguile,
You now suppose me all this time in sport,
And please yourself with this conceit the while.
Ye shallow cens'rers! sometimes, see ye not,
In greatest perils some men pleasant be,
Where fame by death is only to be got,
They resolute! So stands the case with me.
Where other men in depth of passion cry,
I laugh at fortune, as in jest to die.

IDEA XXV

O, why should nature niggardly restrain
That foreign nations relish not our tongue?
Else should my lines glide on the waves of Rhine,
And crown the Pyren's with my living song.
But bounded thus, to Scotland get you forth!
Thence take you wing unto the Orcades!
There let my verse get glory in the north,
Making my sighs to thaw the frozen seas.
And let the bards within that Irish isle,
To whom my Muse with fiery wings shall pass,
Call back the stiff-necked rebels from exile,
And mollify the slaughtering gallowglass;
And when my flowing numbers they rehearse,
Let wolves and bears be charmèd with my verse.

IDEA XXVI - TO DESPAIR

I ever love where never hope appears,
Yet hope draws on my never-hoping care,
And my life's hope would die but for despair;
My never certain joy breeds ever certain fears.
Uncertain dread gives wings unto my hope;
Yet my hope's wings are laden so with fear
As they cannot ascend to my hope's sphere,
Though fear gives them more than a heavenly scope.
Yet this large room is bounded with despair,
So my love is still fettered with vain hope,
And liberty deprives him of his scope,
And thus am I imprisoned in the air.
Then, sweet despair, awhile hold up thy head,
Or all my hope for sorrow will be dead.

IDEA XXVII

Is not love here as 'tis in other climes,
And differeth it as do the several nations?
Or hath it lost the virtue with the times,
Or in this island alt'reth with the fashions?
Or have our passions lesser power than theirs,
Who had less art them lively to express?
Is nature grown less powerful in their heirs,
Or in our fathers did she more transgress?
I am sure my sighs come from a heart as true
As any man's that memory can boast,

And my respects and services to you,
Equal with his that loves his mistress most.
Or nature must be partial in my cause,
Or only you do violate her laws.

IDEA XXVIII

To such as say thy love I overprize,
And do not stick to term my praises folly,
Against these folks that think themselves so wise,
I thus oppose my reason's forces wholly:
Though I give more than well affords my state,
In which expense the most suppose me vain
Which yields them nothing at the easiest rate,
Yet at this price returns me treble gain;
They value not, unskilful how to use,
And I give much because I gain thereby.
I that thus take or they that thus refuse,
Whether are these deceivèd then, or I?
In everything I hold this maxim still,
The circumstance doth make it good or ill.

IDEA XXIX - TO THE SENSES

When conquering love did first my heart assail,
Unto mine aid I summoned every sense,
Doubting if that proud tyrant should prevail,
My heart should suffer for mine eyes' offence.
But he with beauty first corrupted sight,
My hearing bribed with her tongue's harmony,
My taste by her sweet lips drawn with delight,
My smelling won with her breath's spicery,
But when my touching came to play his part,
The king of senses, greater than the rest,
He yields love up the keys unto my heart,
And tells the others how they should be blest.
And thus by those of whom I hoped for aid,
To cruel love my soul was first betrayed.

IDEA XXX - TO THE VESTALS

Those priests which first the vestal fire begun,
Which might be borrowed from no earthly flame,
Devised a vessel to receive the sun,
Being stedfastly opposèd to the same;

Where with sweet wood laid curiously by art,
On which the sun might by reflection beat,
Receiving strength for every secret part,
The fuel kindled with celestial heat.
Thy blessèd eyes, the sun which lights this fire,
My holy thoughts, they be the vestal flame,
Thy precious odours be my chaste desires,
My breast's the vessel which includes the same;
Thou art my Vesta, thou my goddess art,
Thy hallowed temple only is my heart.

IDEA XXXI - TO THE CRITICS

Methinks I see some crooked mimic jeer,
And tax my Muse with this fantastic grace;
Turning my papers asks, "What have we here?"
Making withal some filthy antic face.
I fear no censure nor what thou canst say,
Nor shall my spirit one jot of vigour lose.
Think'st thou, my wit shall keep the packhorse way,
That every dudgeon low invention goes?
Since sonnets thus in bundles are imprest,
And every drudge doth dull our satiate ear,
Think'st thou my love shall in those rags be drest
That every dowdy, every trull doth wear?
Up to my pitch no common judgment flies;
I scorn all earthly dung-bred scarabies.

IDEA XXXII - TO THE RIVER ANKOR

Our floods' queen, Thames, for ships and swans is crowned,
And stately Severn for her shore is praised;
The crystal Trent for fords and fish renowned,
And Avon's fame to Albion's cliff is raised.
Carlegion Chester vaunts her holy Dee;
York many wonders of her Ouse can tell;
The Peak, her Dove, whose banks so fertile be;
And Kent will say her Medway doth excel.
Cotswold commends her Isis to the Thame;
Our northern borders boast of Tweed's fair flood;
Our western parts extol their Wilis' fame;
And the old Lea brags of the Danish blood.
Arden's sweet Ankor, let thy glory be,
That fair Idea only lives by thee!

IDEA XXXIII - TO IMAGINATION

Whilst yet mine eyes do surfeit with delight,
My woful heart imprisoned in my breast,
Wisheth to be transformèd to my sight,
That it like those by looking might be blest.
But whilst mine eyes thus greedily do gaze,
Finding their objects over-soon depart,
These now the other's happiness do praise,
Wishing themselves that they had been my heart,
That eyes were heart, or that the heart were eyes,
As covetous the other's use to have.
But finding nature their request denies,
This to each other mutually they crave;
That since the one cannot the other be,
That eyes could think of that my heart could see.

IDEA XXXIV - TO ADMIRATION

Marvel not, love, though I thy power admire,
Ravished a world beyond the farthest thought,
And knowing more than ever hath been taught,
That I am only starved in my desire.
Marvel not, love, though I thy power admire,
Aiming at things exceeding all perfection,
To wisdom's self to minister direction,
That I am only starved in my desire.
Marvel not, love, though I thy power admire,
Though my conceit I further seem to bend
Than possibly invention can extend,
And yet am only starved in my desire.
If thou wilt wonder, here's the wonder, love,
That this to me doth yet no wonder prove.

IDEA XXXV - TO MIRACLE

Some misbelieving and profane in love,
When I do speak of miracles by thee,
May say that thou art flatterèd by me,
Who only write my skill in verse to prove
See miracles, ye unbelieving, see!
A dumb-born Muse made to express the mind,
A cripple hand to write, yet lame by kind,
One by thy name, the other touching thee.
Blind were mine eyes, till they were seen of thine;
And mine ears deaf by thy fame healèd be;

My vices cured by virtues sprung from thee;
My hopes revived which long in grave had lien.
All unclean thoughts, foul spirits, cast out in me,
Only by virtue that proceeds from thee.

IDEA XXXVI - CUPID CONJURED

Thou purblind boy, since thou hast been so slack
To wound her heart whose eyes have wounded me
And suffered her to glory in my wrack,
Thus to my aid I lastly conjure thee!
By hellish Styx, by which the Thund'rer swears,
By thy fair mother's unavoided power,
By Hecate's names, by Proserpine's sad tears,
When she was wrapt to the infernal bower!
By thine own lovèd Psyche, by the fires
Spent on thine altars flaming up to heaven,
By all true lovers' sighs, vows, and desires,
By all the wounds that ever thou hast given;
I conjure thee by all that I have named,
To make her love, or, Cupid, be thou damned!

IDEA XXXVII

Dear, why should you command me to my rest,
When now the night doth summon all to sleep?
Methinks this time becometh lovers best;
Night was ordained together friends to keep.
How happy are all other living things,
Which though the day disjoin by several flight,
The quiet evening yet together brings,
And each returns unto his love at night!
O thou that art so courteous else to all,
Why shouldst thou, Night, abuse me only thus,
That every creature to his kind dost call,
And yet 'tis thou dost only sever us?
Well could I wish it would be ever day,
If when night comes, you bid me go away.

IDEA XXXVIII

Sitting alone, love bids me go and write;
Reason plucks back, commanding me to stay,
Boasting that she doth still direct the way,
Or else love were unable to indite.

Love growing angry, vexèd at the spleen,
And scorning reason's maimèd argument,
Straight taxeth reason, wanting to invent
Where she with love conversing hath not been.
Reason reproachèd with this coy disdain,
Despiteth love, and laugheth at her folly;
And love contemning reason's reason wholly,
Thought it in weight too light by many a grain.
Reason put back doth out of sight remove,
And love alone picks reason out of love.

IDEA XXXIX

Some, when in rhyme they of their loves do tell,
With flames and lightnings their exordiums paint.
Some call on heaven, some invocate on hell,
And Fates and Furies, with their woes acquaint.
Elizium is too high a seat for me,
I will not come in Styx or Phlegethon,
The thrice-three Muses but too wanton be,
Like they that lust, I care not, I will none.
Spiteful Erinnys frights me with her looks,
My manhood dares not with foul Ate mell,
I quake to look on Hecate's charming books,
I still fear bugbears in Apollo's cell.
I pass not for Minerva, nor Astrea,
Only I call on my divine Idea!

IDEA XL

My heart the anvil where my thoughts do beat,
My words the hammers fashioning my desire,
My breast the forge including all the heat,
Love is the fuel which maintains the fire;
My sighs the bellows which the flame increaseth,
Filling mine ears with noise and nightly groaning;
Toiling with pain, my labour never ceaseth,
In grievous passions my woes still bemoaning;
My eyes with tears against the fire striving,
Whose scorching gleed my heart to cinders turneth;
But with those drops the flame again reviving,
Still more and more it to my torment burneth,
With Sisyphus thus do I roll the stone,
And turn the wheel with damnèd Ixion.

IDEA XLI - LOVE'S LUNACY

Why do I speak of joy or write of love,
When my heart is the very den of horror,
And in my soul the pains of hell I prove,
With all his torments and infernal terror?
What should I say? what yet remains to do?
My brain is dry with weeping all too long;
My sighs be spent in utt'ring of my woe,
And I want words wherewith to tell my wrong.
But still distracted in love's lunacy,
And bedlam-like thus raving in my grief,
Now rail upon her hair, then on her eye,
Now call her goddess, then I call her thief;
Now I deny her, then I do confess her,
Now do I curse her, then again I bless her.

IDEA XLII

Some men there be which like my method well,
And much commend the strangeness of my vein;
Some say I have a passing pleasing strain,
Some say that in my humour I excel.
Some who not kindly relish my conceit,
They say, as poets do, I use to feign,
And in bare words paint out by passions' pain.
Thus sundry men their sundry minds repeat.
I pass not, I, how men affected be,
Nor who commends or discommends my verse!
It pleaseth me if I my woes rehearse,
And in my lines if she my love may see.
Only my comfort still consists in this,
Writing her praise I cannot write amiss.

IDEA XLIII

Why should your fair eyes with such sov'reign grace
Disperse their rays on every vulgar spirit,
Whilst I in darkness in the self-same place,
Get not one glance to recompense my merit?
So doth the plowman gaze the wand'ring star,
And only rest contented with the light,
That never learned what constellations are,
Beyond the bent of his unknowing sight.
O why should beauty, custom to obey,
To their gross sense apply herself so ill!

Would God I were as ignorant as they,
When I am made unhappy by my skill,
Only compelled on this poor good to boast!
Heavens are not kind to them that know them most.

IDEA XLIV

Whilst thus my pen strives to eternise thee,
Age rules my lines with wrinkles in my face,
Where in the map of all my misery
Is modelled out the world of my disgrace;
Whilst in despite of tyrannising times,
Medea-like, I make thee young again,
Proudly thou scorn'st my world-outwearing rhymes,
And murther'st virtue with thy coy disdain;
And though in youth my youth untimely perish,
To keep thee from oblivion and the grave,
Ensuing ages yet my rhymes shall cherish,
Where I intombed my better part shall save;
And though this earthly body fade and die,
My name shall mount upon eternity.

IDEA XLV

Muses which sadly sit about my chair,
Drowned in the tears extorted by my lines;
With heavy sighs whilst thus I break the air,
Painting my passions in these sad designs,
Since she disdains to bless my happy verse,
The strong built trophies to her living fame,
Ever henceforth my bosom be your hearse,
Wherein the world shall now entomb her name.
Enclose my music, you poor senseless walls,
Sith she is deaf and will not hear my moans;
Soften yourselves with every tear that falls,
Whilst I like Orpheus sing to trees and stones,
Which with my plaint seem yet with pity moved,
Kinder than she whom I so long have loved.

IDEA XLVI

Plain-pathed experience, the unlearnèd's guide,
Her simple followers evidently shows
Sometimes what schoolmen scarcely can decide,
Nor yet wise reason absolutely knows;

In making trial of a murder wrought,
If the vile actors of the heinous deed
Near the dead body happily be brought,
Oft 't hath been proved the breathless corse will bleed.
She coming near, that my poor heart hath slain,
Long since departed, to the world no more,
The ancient wounds no longer can contain,
But fall to bleeding as they did before.
But what of this? Should she to death be led,
It furthers justice but helps not the dead.

IDEA XLVII

In pride of wit, when high desire of fame
Gave life and courage to my lab'ring pen,
And first the sound and virtue of my name
Won grace and credit in the ears of men,
With those the throngèd theatres that press,
I in the circuit for the laurel strove,
Where the full praise I freely must confess,
In heat of blood a modest mind might move;
With shouts and claps at every little pause,
When the proud round on every side hath rung,
Sadly I sit unmoved with the applause,
As though to me it nothing did belong.
No public glory vainly I pursue;
All that I seek is to eternise you.

IDEA XLVIII

Cupid, I hate thee, which I'd have thee know;
A naked starveling ever mayst thou be!
Poor rogue, go pawn thy fascia and thy bow
For some poor rags wherewith to cover thee;
Or if thou'lt not thy archery forbear,
To some base rustic do thyself prefer,
And when corn's sown or grown into the ear,
Practice thy quiver and turn crowkeeper;
Or being blind, as fittest for the trade,
Go hire thyself some bungling harper's boy;
They that are blind are minstrels often made,
So mayst thou live to thy fair mother's joy;
That whilst with Mars she holdeth her old way,
Thou, her blind son, mayst sit by them and play.

IDEA XLIX

Thou leaden brain, which censur'st what I write,
And sayst my lines be dull and do not move,
I marvel not thou feel'st not my delight,
Which never felt'st my fiery touch of love;
But thou whose pen hath like a packhorse served,
Whose stomach unto gall hath turned thy food,
Whose senses like poor prisoners, hunger-starved
Whose grief hath parched thy body, dried thy blood;
Thou which hast scornèd life and hated death,
And in a moment, mad, sober, glad, and sorry;
Thou which hast banned thy thoughts and curst thy birth
With thousand plagues more than in purgatory;
Thou thus whose spirit love in his fire refines,
Come thou and read, admire, applaud my lines!

IDEA L

As in some countries far remote from hence,
The wretched creature destinèd to die,
Having the judgment due to his offence,
By surgeons begged, their art on him to try,
Which on the living work without remorse,
First make incision on each mastering vein,
Then staunch the bleeding, then transpierce the corse,
And with their balms recure the wounds again,
Then poison and with physic him restore;
Not that they fear the hopeless man to kill,
But their experience to increase the more:
Even so my mistress works upon my ill,
By curing me and killing me each hour,
Only to show her beauty's sovereign power.

IDEA LI

Calling to mind since first my love begun,
Th'uncertain times, oft varying in their course,
How things still unexpectedly have run,
As't please the Fates by their resistless force;
Lastly, mine eyes amazedly have seen
Essex's great fall, Tyrone his peace to gain,
The quiet end of that long living Queen,
This King's fair entrance, and our peace with Spain,
We and the Dutch at length ourselves to sever;
Thus the world doth and evermore shall reel;

Yet to my goddess am I constant ever,
Howe'er blind Fortune turn her giddy wheel;
Though heaven and earth prove both to me untrue,
Yet am I still inviolate to you.

IDEA LII

What dost thou mean to cheat me of my heart,
To take all mine and give me none again?
Or have thine eyes such magic or that art
That what they get they ever do retain?
Play not the tyrant but take some remorse;
Rebate thy spleen if but for pity's sake;
Or cruel, if thou can'st not, let us scorse,
And for one piece of thine my whole heart take.
But what of pity do I speak to thee,
Whose breast is proof against complaint or prayer?
Or can I think what my reward shall be
From that proud beauty which was my betrayer!
What talk I of a heart when thou hast none?
Or if thou hast, it is a flinty one.

IDEA LIII - ANOTHER TO THE RIVER ANKOR

Clear Ankor, on whose silver-sanded shore,
My soul-shrined saint, my fair Idea lives;
O blessèd brook, whose milk-white swans adore
Thy crystal stream, refinèd by her eyes,
Where sweet myrrh-breathing Zephyr in the spring
Gently distils his nectar-dropping showers,
Where nightingales in Arden sit and sing
Amongst the dainty dew-impearlèd flowers;
Say thus, fair brook, when thou shalt see thy queen,
"Lo, here thy shepherd spent his wand'ring years
And in these shades, dear nymph, he oft hath been;
And here to thee he sacrificed his tears."
Fair Arden, thou my Tempe art alone,
And thou, sweet Ankor, art my Helicon!

IDEA LIV

Yet read at last the story of my woe,
The dreary abstracts of my endless cares,
With my life's sorrow interlinèd so,
Smoked with my sighs, and blotted with my tears,

The sad memorials of my miseries,
Penned in the grief of mine afflicted ghost,
My life's complaint in doleful elegies,
With so pure love as time could never boast.
Receive the incense which I offer here,
By my strong faith ascending to thy fame,
My zeal, my hope, my vows, my praise, my prayer,
My soul's oblations to thy sacred name;
Which name my Muse to highest heavens shall raise,
By chaste desire, true love, and virtuous praise.

IDEA LV

My fair, if thou wilt register my love,
A world of volumes shall thereof arise;
Preserve my tears, and thou thyself shall prove
A second flood down raining from mine eyes;
Note but my sighs, and thine eyes shall behold
The sunbeams smothered with immortal smoke;
And if by thee my prayers may be enrolled,
They heaven and earth to pity shall provoke.
Look thou into my breast, and thou shalt see
Chaste holy vows for my soul's sacrifice,
That soul, sweet maid, which so hath honoured thee,
Erecting trophies to thy sacred eyes,
Those eyes to my heart shining ever bright,
When darkness hath obscured each other light.

IDEA LVI - AN ALLUSION TO THE EAGLETS

When like an eaglet I first found my love,
For that the virtue I thereof would know,
Upon the nest I set it forth to prove
If it were of that kingly kind or no;
But it no sooner saw my sun appear,
But on her rays with open eyes it stood,
To show that I had hatched it for the air,
And rightly came from that brave mounting brood;
And when the plumes were summed with sweet desire,
To prove the pinions it ascends the skies;
Do what I could, it needsly would aspire
To my soul's sun, those two celestial eyes.
Thus from my breast, where it was bred alone,
It after thee is like an eaglet flown.

IDEA LVII

You best discerned of my mind's inward eyes,
And yet your graces outwardly divine,
Whose dear remembrance in my bosom lies,
Too rich a relic for so poor a shrine;
You, in whom nature chose herself to view,
When she her own perfection would admire;
Bestowing all her excellence on you,
At whose pure eyes Love lights his hallowed fire;
Even as a man that in some trance hath seen
More than his wond'ring utterance can unfold,
That rapt in spirit in better worlds hath been,
So must your praise distractedly be told;
Most of all short when I would show you most,
In your perfections so much am I lost.

IDEA LVIII

In former times, such as had store of coin,
In wars at home or when for conquests bound,
For fear that some their treasure should purloin,
Gave it to keep to spirits within the ground;
And to attend it them as strongly tied
Till they returned. Home when they never came,
Such as by art to get the same have tried,
From the strong spirit by no means force the same.
Nearer men come, that further flies away,
Striving to hold it strongly in the deep.
Ev'n as this spirit, so you alone do play
With those rich beauties Heav'n gives you to keep;
Pity so left to th' coldness of your blood,
Not to avail you nor do others good.

IDEA LIX - TO PROVERBS

As Love and I late harboured in one inn,
With Proverbs thus each other entertain.
"In love there is no lack," thus I begin:
"Fair words make fools," replieth he again.
"Who spares to speak, doth spare to speed," quoth I.
"As well," saith he, "too forward as too slow."
"Fortune assists the boldest," I reply.
"A hasty man," quoth he, "ne'er wanted woe!"
"Labour is light, where love," quoth I, "doth pay."
Saith he, "Light burden's heavy, if far born."

Quoth I, "The main lost, cast the by away!"
"You have spun a fair thread," he replies in scorn.
And having thus awhile each other thwarted,
Fools as we met, so fools again we parted.

IDEA LX

Define my weal, and tell the joys of heaven;
Express my woes and show the pains of hell;
Declare what fate unlucky stars have given,
And ask a world upon my life to dwell;
Make known the faith that fortune could no move,
Compare my worth with others' base desert,
Let virtue be the touchstone of my love,
So may the heavens read wonders in my heart;
Behold the clouds which have eclipsed my sun,
And view the crosses which my course do let;
Tell me, if ever since the world begun
So fair a rising had so foul a set?
And see if time, if he would strive to prove,
Can show a second to so pure a love.

IDEA LXI

Since there's no help, come let us kiss and part,
Nay I have done, you get no more of me;
And I am glad, yea glad with all my heart,
That thus so cleanly I myself can free;
Shakes hands for ever, cancel all our vows,
And when we meet at any time again,
Be it not seen in either of our brows
That we one jot of former love retain.
Now at the last gasp of Love's latest breath,
When his pulse failing, Passion speechless lies,
When Faith is kneeling by his bed of death,
And Innocence is closing up his eyes:
Now if thou wouldst, when all have given him over,
From death to life thou might'st him yet recover!

IDEA LXII

When first I ended, then I first began;
Then more I travelled further from my rest.
Where most I lost, there most of all I won;
Pinèd with hunger, rising from a feast.

Methinks I fly, yet want I legs to go,
Wise in conceit, in act a very sot,
Ravished with joy amidst a hell of woe,
What most I seem that surest am I not.
I build my hopes a world above the sky,
Yet with the mole I creep into the earth;
In plenty I am starved with penury,
And yet I surfeit in the greatest dearth.
I have, I want, despair, and yet desire,
Burned in a sea of ice, and drowned amidst a fire.

IDEA LXIII

Truce, gentle Love, a parley now I crave,
Methinks 'tis long since first these wars begun;
Nor thou, nor I, the better yet can have;
Bad is the match where neither party won.
I offer free conditions of fair peace,
My heart for hostage that it shall remain.
Discharge our forces, here let malice cease,
So for my pledge thou give me pledge again.
Or if no thing but death will serve thy turn,
Still thirsting for subversion of my state,
Do what thou canst, raze, massacre, and burn;
Let the world see the utmost of thy hate;
I send defiance, since if overthrown,
Thou vanquishing, the conquest is mine own.

Michael Drayton – A Short Biography by Cyril Brett

Michael Drayton was born in 1563, at Hartshill, near Atherstone, in Warwickshire.

He became a page to Sir Henry Goodere, at Polesworth Hall: his own words give the best picture of his early years here. His education would seem to have been good, but ordinary; and it is very doubtful if he ever went to a university. Besides the authors mentioned in the Epistle to Henry Reynolds, he was certainly familiar with Ovid and Horace, and possibly with Catullus: while there seems no reason to doubt that he read Greek, though it is quite true that his references to Greek authors do not prove any first-hand acquaintance. He understood French, and read Rabelais and the French sonneteers, and he seems to have been acquainted with Italian. His knowledge of English literature was wide, and his judgement good: but his chief bent lay towards the history, legendary and otherwise, of his native country, and his vast stores of learning on this subject bore fruit in the Poly-Olbion.

While still at Polesworth, Drayton fell in love with his patron's younger daughter, Anne; and, though she married, in 1596, Sir Henry Raynsford of Clifford, Drayton continued his devotion to her for many years, and also became an intimate friend of her husband's, writing a sincere elegy on his death.

About February, 1591, Drayton paid a visit to London, and published his first work, the Harmony of the Church, a series of paraphrases from the Old Testament, in fourteen-syllabled verse of no particular vigour or grace. This book was immediately suppressed by order of Archbishop Whitgift, possibly because it was supposed to savour of Puritanism. The author, however, published another edition in 1610; indeed, he seems to have had a fondness for this style of work; for in 1604 he published a dull poem, Moyses in a Map of his Miracles, re-issued in 1630 as Moses his Birth and Miracles. Accompanying this piece, in 1630, were two other 'Divine poems': Noah's Floud, and David and Goliath. Noah's Floud is, in part, one of Drayton's happiest attempts at the catalogue style of bestiary; and Mr. Elton finds in it some foreshadowing of the manner of Paradise Lost. But, as a whole, Drayton's attempts in this direction deserve the oblivion into which they, in common with the similar productions of other authors, have fallen. In the dedication and preface to the Harmony of the Church are some of the few traces of Euphuism shown in Drayton's work; passages in the Heroical Epistles also occur to the mind He was always averse to affectation, literary or otherwise, and in Elegy VIII deliberately condemns Lyly's fantastic style.

Probably before Drayton went up to London, Sir Henry Goodere saw that he would stand in need of a patron more powerful than the master of Polesworth, and introduced him to the Earl and Countess of Bedford. Those who believe Drayton to have been a Pope in petty spite, identify the 'Idea' of his earlier poems with Lucy, Countess of Bedford; though they are forced to acknowledge as self-evident that the 'Idea' of his later work is Anne, Lady Raynsford. They then proceed to say that Drayton, after consistently honouring the Countess in his verse for twelve years, abruptly transferred his allegiance, not forgetting to heap foul abuse on his former patroness, out of pique at some temporary withdrawal of favour. Not only is this directly contrary to all we know and can infer of Drayton's character, but Mr. Elton has decisively disproved it by a summary of bibliographical and other evidence. Into the question it is here unnecessary to enter, and it has been mentioned only because it alone, of the many Drayton-controversies, has cast any slur on the poet's reputation.

In 1593, Drayton published Idea, the Shepherds Garland, in nine Eclogues; in 1606 he added a tenth, the best of all, to the new edition, and rearranged the order, so that the new eclogue became the ninth. In these Pastorals, while following the Shepherds Calendar in many ways, he already displays something of the sturdy independence which characterized him through life. He abandons Spenser's quasi-rustic dialect, and, while keeping to most of the pastoral conventions, such as the singing-match and threnody, he contrives to introduce something of a more natural and homely strain. He keeps the political allusions, notably in the Eclogue containing the song in praise of Beta, who is, of course, Queen Elizabeth. But an over-bold remark in the last line of that song was struck out in 1606; and the new eclogue has no political reference. He is not ashamed to allude directly to Spenser; and indeed his direct debts are limited to a few scattered phrases, as in the Ballad of Dowsabel. Almost to the end of his literary career, Drayton mentions Spenser with reverence and praise.

It is in the songs interspersed in the Eclogues that Drayton's best work at this time is to be found: already his metrical versatility is discernible; for though he doubtless remembered the many varieties of metre employed by Spenser in the Calendar, his verses already bear a stamp of their own. The long but impetuous lines, such as 'Trim up her golden tresses with Apollo's sacred tree', afford a striking contrast to the archaic romance-metre, derived from Sir Thopas and its fellows, which appears in Dowsabel, and it again to the melancholy, murmuring cadences of the lament for Elphin. It must, however, be confessed that certain of the songs in the 1593 edition were full of recondite conceits and laboured antitheses, and were rightly struck out, to be replaced by lovelier poems, in the edition of 1606. The song to Beta was printed in Englands Helicon, 1600; here, for the first time, appeared the song of Dead

Love, and for the only time, Rowlands Madrigal. In these songs, Drayton offends least in grammar, always a weak point with him; in the body of the Eclogues, in the earlier Sonnets, in the Odes, occur the most extraordinary and perplexing inversions. Quite the most striking feature of the Eclogues, especially in their later form, is their bold attempt at greater realism, at a breaking-away from the conventional images and scenery.

Having paid his tribute to one poetic fashion, Drayton in 1594 fell in with the prevailing craze for sonneteering, and published Ideas Mirrour, a series of fifty-one 'amours' or sonnets, with two prefatory poems, one by Drayton and one by an unknown, signing himself Gorbo il fidele. The title of these poems Drayton possibly borrowed from the French sonneteer, de Pontoux: in their style much recollection of Sidney, Constable, and Daniel is traceable. They are ostensibly addressed to his mistress, and some of them are genuine in feeling; but many are merely imitative exercises in conceit; some, apparently, trials in metre. These amours were again printed, with the title of 'sonnets', in 1599, 1600, 1602, 1603, 1605, 1608, 1610, 1613, 1619, and 1631, during the poet's lifetime. It is needless here to discuss whether Drayton were the 'rival poet' to Shakespeare, whether these sonnets were really addressed to a man, or merely to the ideal Platonic beauty; for those who are interested in these points, I subjoin references to the sonnets which touch upon them. From the prentice-work evident in many of the Amours, it would seem that certain of them are among Drayton's earliest poems; but others show a craftsman not meanly advanced in his art. Nevertheless, with few exceptions, this first 'bundle of sonnets' consists rather of trials of skill, bubbles of the mind; most of his sonnets which strike the reader as touched or penetrated with genuine passion belong to the editions from 1599 onwards; implying that his love for Anne Goodere, if at all represented in these poems, grew with his years, for the 'love-parting' is first found in the edition of 1619. But for us the question should not be, are these sonnets genuine representations of the personal feeling of the poet? but rather, how far do they arouse or echo in us as individuals the universal passion? There are at least some of Drayton's sonnets which possess a direct, instant, and universal appeal, by reason of their simple force and straightforward ring; and not in virtue of any subtle charm of sound and rhythm, or overmastering splendour of diction or thought. Ornament vanishes, and soberness and simplicity increase, as we proceed in the editions of the sonnets. Drayton's chief attempt in the jewelled or ornamental style appeared in 1595, with the title of Endimion and Phoebe, and was, in a sense, an imitation of Marlowe's Hero and Leander. Hero and Leander is, as Swinburne says, a shrine of Parian marble, illumined from within by a clear flame of passion; while Endimion and Phoebe is rather a curiously wrought tapestry, such as that in Mortimer's Tower, woven in splendid and harmonious colours, wherein, however, the figures attain no clearness or subtlety of outline, and move in semi-conventional scenery. It is, none the less, graceful and impressive, and of a like musical fluency with other poems of its class, such as Venus and Adonis, or Salmacis and Hermaphrodius. Parts of it were re-set and spoilt in a 1606 publication of Drayton's, called The Man in the Moone.

In 1593 and 1594 Drayton also published his earliest pieces on the mediaeval theme of the 'Falls of the Illustrious'; they were Peirs Gavesson and Matilda the faire and chaste daughter of the Lord Robert Fitzwater. Here Drayton followed in the track of Boccaccio, Lydgate, and the Mirror for Magistrates, walking in the way which Chaucer had derided in his Monkes Tale: and with only too great fidelity does Drayton adapt himself to the dullnesses of his model: fine rhetoric is not altogether wanting, and there is, of course, the consciousness that these subjects deal with the history of his beloved country, but neither these, nor Robert, Duke of Normandy (1596), nor Great Cromwell, Earl of Essex (1607 and 1609), nor the Miseries of Margaret (1627) can escape the charge of tediousness. England's Heroical Epistles were first published in 1597, and other editions, of 1598, 1599, and 1602, contain new epistles. These are Drayton's first attempt to strike out a new and original vein of English poetry: they are a series of letters, modelled on Ovid's Heroides, addressed by various pairs of lovers, famous in English history, to each other, and arranged in chronological order, from Henry II and Rosamond to Lady Jane Grey and Lord Guilford Dudley. They are, in a sense, the most important of Drayton's writings, and they have certainly been the most popular, up to the early nineteenth century. In these poems Drayton foreshadowed, and probably inspired, the smooth style of Fairfax, Waller, and Dryden. The metre, the grammar, and the thought, are all perfectly easy to follow, even though he employs many of the Ovidian 'turns' and 'clenches'. A certain attempt at realization of the different characters is observable, but the poems are fine rhetorical exercises rather than realizations of the dramatic and passionate possibilities of their themes. In 1596, Drayton, as we have seen, published the Mortimeriados, a kind of epic, with Mortimer as its hero, of the wars between King Edward II and the Barons. It was written in the seven-line stanza of Chaucer's Troilus and Cressida and Spenser's Hymns. On its republication in 1603, with the title of the Barons' Wars, the metre was changed to ottava rima, and Drayton showed, in an excellent preface, that he fully appreciated the principles and the subtleties of the metrical art. While possessing many fine passages, the Barons' Wars is somewhat dull, lacking much of the poetry of the older version; and does not escape from Drayton's own criticism of Daniel's Chronicle Poems: 'too much historian in verse, ... His rhymes were smooth, his metres well did close, But yet his manner better fitted prose'. The description of Mortimer's Tower in the sixth book recalls the ornate style of Endimion and Phoebe, while the fifth book, describing the miseries of King Edward, is the most moving and dramatic. But there is a general lifelessness and lack of movement for which these purple passages barely atone. The cause of the production of so many chronicle poems about this time has been supposed to be the desire of showing the horrors of civil war, at a time when the queen was growing old, and no successor had, as it seemed, been accepted. Also they were a kind of parallel to the Chronicle Play; and Drayton, in any case even if we grant him to have been influenced by the example of Daniel, never needed much incentive to treat a national theme.

About this time, we find Drayton writing for the stage. It seems unnecessary here to discuss whether the writing of plays is evidence of Drayton's poverty, or his versatility; but the fact remains that he had a hand in the production of about twenty. Of these, the only one which certainly survives is The first part of the true and honorable historie, of the life of Sir John Oldcastle, the good Lord Cobham, &c. It is practically impossible to distinguish Drayton's share in this curious play, and it does not, therefore, materially assist the elucidation of the question whether he had any dramatic feeling or skill. It can be safely affirmed that the dramatic instinct was nor uppermost in his mind; he was a Seneca rather than a Euripides: but to deny him all dramatic idea, as does Dr. Whitaker, is too severe. There is decided, if slender, dramatic skill and feeling in certain of the Nymphals. Drayton's persons are usually, it must be said, rather figures in a tableau, or series of tableaux; but in the second and seventh Nymphals, and occasionally in the tenth, there is real dramatic movement. Closely connected with this question is the consideration of humour, which is wrongly denied to Drayton. Humour is observable first, perhaps, in the Owle (1604); then in the Ode to his Rival (1619); and later in the Nymphidia, Shepheards Sirena, and Muses Elyzium. The second Nymphal shows us the quiet laughter, the humorous twinkle, with which Drayton writes at times. The subject is an [Greek: agôn] or contest between two shepherds for the affections of a nymph called Lirope: Lalus is a vale-bred swain, of refined and elegant manners, skilled, nevertheless, in all manly sports and exercises; Cleon, no less a master in physical prowess, was nurtured by a hind in the mountains; the contrast between their manners is admirably sustained: Cleon is rough, inclined to be rude and scoffing, totally without tact, even where his mistress is concerned. Lalus remembers her upbringing and her tastes; he makes no unnecessary or ostentatious display of wealth; his gifts are simple and charming, while Cleon's are so grotesquely unsuited to a swain, that it is tempting to suppose that Drayton was quietly satirizing Marlowe's Passionate Shepherd. Lirope listens gravely to the swains in turn, and makes demure but provoking answers, raising each to the height of hope, and then casting them both down into the depths of despair; finally she refuses both, yet without altogether killing hope. Her first answer is a good specimen of her banter and of Drayton's humour.

On the accession of James I, Drayton hastened to greet the King with a somewhat laboured song To the Maiestie of King James; but this poem was apparently considered to be premature: he cried Vivat Rex, without having said, Mortua est eheu Regina, and accordingly he suffered the penalty of his 'forward pen', and was severely neglected by King and Court. Throughout James's reign a darker and more satirical mood possesses Drayton, intruding at times even into his strenuous recreation-ground, the Poly-Olbion, and manifesting itself more directly in his satires, the Owle (1604), the Moon-Calfe (1627), the Man in the Moone (1606), and his verse-letters and elegies; while his disappointment with the times, the country, and the King, flashes out occasionally even in the Odes, and is heard in his last publication, the Muses Elizium (1630). To counterbalance the disappointment in his hopes from the King, Drayton found a new and life-long friend in Walter Aston, of Tixall, in Staffordshire; this gentleman was created Knight of the Bath by James, and made Drayton one of his esquires. By Aston's 'continual bounty' the poet was able to devote himself almost entirely to more congenial literary work; for, while Meres speaks of the Poly-Olbion in 1598, and we may easily see that Drayton had the idea of that work at least as early as 1594, yet he cannot have been able to give much time to it till now. Nevertheless, the 'declining and corrupt times' worked on Drayton's mind and grieved and darkened his soul, for we must remember that he was perfectly prosperous then and was not therefore incited to satire by bodily want or distress.

In 1604 he published the Owle, a mild satire, under the form of a moral fable of government, reminding the reader a little of the Parlement of Foules. The Man in the Moone (1606) is partly a recension of Endimion and Phoebe, but is a heterogeneous mass of weakly satire, of no particular merit. The Moon-Calfe (1627) is Drayton's most savage and misanthropic excursion into the region of Satire; in which, though occasionally nobly ironic, he is more usually coarse and blustering, in the style of Marston. In 1605 Drayton brought out his first 'collected poems', from which the Eclogues and the Owle are omitted; and in 1606 he published his Poemes Lyrick and Pastorall, Odes, Eglogs, The Man in the Moone. Of these the Eglogs are a recension of the Shepherd's Garland of 1593: we have already spoken of The Man in the Moone. The Odes are by far the most important and striking feature of the book. In the preface, Drayton professes to be following Pindar, Anacreon, and Horace, though, as he modestly implies, at a great distance. Under the title of Odes he includes a variety of subjects, and a variety of metres; ranging from an Ode to his Harp or to his Criticks, to a Ballad of Agincourt, or a poem on the Rose compared with his Mistress. In the edition of 1619 appeared several more Odes, including some of the best; while many of the others underwent careful revision, notably the Ballad. 'Sing wee the Rose,' perhaps because of its unintelligibility, and the Ode to his friend John Savage, perhaps because too closely imitated from Horace, were omitted. Drayton was not the first to use the term Ode for a lyrical poem, in English: Soothern in 1584, and Daniel in 1592 had preceded him; but he was the first to give the name popularity in England, and to lift the kind as Ronsard had lifted it in France; and till the time of Cowper no other English poet showed mastery of the short, staccato measure of the Anacreontic as distinct from the Pindaric Ode. In the Odes Drayton shows to the fullest extent his metrical versatility: he touches the Skeltonic metre, the long ten-syllabled line of the Sacrifice to Apollo; and ascends from the smooth and melodious rhythms of the New Year through the inspiring harp-tones of the Virginian Voyage to the clangour and swing of the Ballad of Agincourt. His grammar is possibly more distorted here than anywhere, but, as Mr. Elton says, 'these are the obstacles of any poet who uses measures of four or six syllables.' His tone throughout is rather that of the harp, as played, perhaps, in Polesworth Hall, than that of any other instrument; but in 1619 Drayton has taken to him the lute of Carew and his compeers. In 1619 the style is lighter, the fancy gayer, more exquisite, more recondite. Most of his few metaphysical conceits are to be found in these later Odes, as in the Heart, the Valentine, and the Crier. In the comparison of the two editions the nobler, if more strained, tone of the earlier is obvious; it is still Elizabethan, in its nobility of ideal and purpose, in its enthusiasm, in its belief and confidence in England and her men; and this even though we catch a glimpse of the Jacobean woe in the Ode to John Savage: the 1619 Odes are of a different world; their spirit is lighter, more insouciant in appearance, though perhaps studiedly so; the rhythms are more fantastic, with less of strength and firmness, though with more of grace and superficial beauty; even the very textual alterations, while usually increasing the grace and the music of the lines, remind the reader that something of the old spontaneity and freshness is gone.

In 1607 and 1609, Drayton published two editions of the last and weakest of his mediaeval poems—the Legend of Great Cromwell; and for the next few years he produced nothing new, only attending to the publication of certain reprints and new editions. During this time, however, he was working steadily at the Poly-Olbion, helped by the patronage of Aston and of Prince Henry. In 1612-13, Drayton burst upon an indifferent world with the first part of the great poem, containing eighteen songs; the title-page will give the best idea of the contents and plan of the book: 'Poly-Olbion or a Chorographicall Description of the Tracts, Riuers, Mountaines, Forests, and other Parts of this renowned Isle of Great Britaine, With intermixture of the most Remarquable Stories, Antiquities, Wonders, Rarityes, Pleasures, and Commodities of the same: Digested in a Poem by Michael Drayton, Esq. With a Table added, for direction to those occurrences of Story and Antiquities, whereunto the Course of the Volume easily leades not.' &c. On this work Drayton had been engaged for nearly the whole of his poetical career. The learning and research displayed in the poem are extraordinary, almost equalling the erudition of Selden in his Annotations to each Song. The first part was, for various reasons, a drug in the market, and Drayton found great difficulty in securing a publisher for the second part. But during the years from 1613 to 1622, he became acquainted with Drummond of Hawthornden through a common friend, Sir William Alexander of Menstry, afterwards Earl of Stirling. In 1618, Drayton starts a correspondence; and towards the end of the year mentions that he is corresponding also with Andro Hart, bookseller, of Edinburgh. The subject of his letter was probably the publication of the Second Part; which Drayton alludes to in a letter of 1619 thus: 'I have done twelve books more, that is from the eighteenth book, which was Kent, if you note it; all the East part and North to the river Tweed; but it lies by me; for the booksellers and I are in terms; they are a company of base knaves, whom I both scorn and kick at.' Finally, in 1622, Drayton got Marriott, Grismand, and Dewe, of London, to take the work, and it was published with a dedication to Prince Charles, who, after his brother's death, had given Drayton patronage. Drayton's preface to the Second Part is well worth quoting:

'To any that will read it. When I first undertook this Poem, or, as some very skilful in this kind have pleased to term it, this Herculean labour, I was by some virtuous friends persuaded, that I should receive much comfort and encouragement therein; and for these reasons; First, that it was a new, clear, way, never before gone by any; then, that it contained all the Delicacies, Delights, and Rarities of this renowned Isle, interwoven with the Histories of the Britons, Saxons, Normans, and the later English: And further that there is scarcely any of the Nobility or Gentry of this land, but that he is in some way or other by his Blood interested therein. But it hath fallen out otherwise; for instead of that comfort, which my noble friends (from the freedom of their spirits) proposed as my due, I have met with barbarous ignorance, and base detraction; such a cloud hath the Devil drawn over the world's judgment, whose opinion is in few years fallen so far below all ballatry, that the lethargy is incurable: nay, some of the Stationers, that had the selling of the First Part of this Poem, because it went not so fast away in the sale, as some of their beastly and abominable trash, (a shame both to our language and nation) have either despitefully left out, or at least carelessly neglected the Epistles to the Readers, and so have cozened the buyers with unperfected books; which these that have undertaken the Second Part, have been forced to amend in the First, for the small number that are yet remaining in their hands. And some of our outlandish, unnatural, English, (I know not how otherwise to express them) stick not to say that there is nothing in this Island worth studying for, and take a great pride to be ignorant in any thing thereof; for these, since they delight in their folly, I wish it may be hereditary from them to their posterity, that their children may be begg'd for fools to the fifth generation, until it may be beyond the memory of man to know that there was ever other of their families: neither can this deter me from going on with Scotland, if means and time do not hinder me, to perform as much as I have promised in my First Song:

Till through the sleepy main, to Thuly I have gone,
And seen the Frozen Isles, the cold Deucalidon,
Amongst whose iron Rocks, grim Saturn yet remains
Bound in those gloomy caves with adamantine chains.

And as for those cattle whereof I spake before, Odi profanum vulgus, et arceo, of which I account them, be they never so great, and so I leave them. To my friends, and the lovers of my labours, I wish all happiness.
Michael Drayton.'

The Poly-Olbion as a whole is easy and pleasant to read; and though in some parts it savours too much of a mere catalogue, yet it has many things truly poetical. The best books are perhaps the XIII, XIV and XV, where he is on his own ground, and therefore naturally at his best. It is interesting to notice how much attention and space he devotes to Wales. He describes not only the 'wonders' but also the fauna and flora of each district; and of the two it would seem that the flowers interested him more. Though he was a keen observer of country sights and sounds (a fact sufficiently attested by the Nymphidia and the Nymphals), it is evident that his interest in most things except flowers was rather momentary or conventional than continuous and heart-felt; but of the flowers he loves to talk, whether he weaves us a garland for the Thame's wedding, or gives us the contents of a maund of simples; and his love, if somewhat homely and unimaginative, is apparent enough. But the main inspiration, as it is the main theme, of the Poly-Olbion is the glory and might and wealth, past, present, and future, of England, her possessions and her folk. Through all this glory, however, we catch the tone of Elizabethan sorrow over the 'Ruines of Time'; grief that all these mighty men and their works will perish and be forgotten, unless the poet makes them live for ever on the lips of men. Drayton's own voluminousness has defeated his purpose, and sunk his poem by its own bulk. Though it is difficult to go so far as Mr. Bullen, and say that the only thing better than a stroll in the Poly-Olbion is one in a Sussex lane, it is still harder to agree with Canon Beeching, that 'there are few beauties on the road', the beauties are many, though of a quietly rural type, and the road, if long and winding, is of good surface, while its cranks constitute much of its charm. It is doubtless, from the outside, an appalling poem in these days of epitomes and monographs, but it certainly deserves to be rescued from oblivion and read.

In 1618 Drayton contributed two Elegies to Henry FitzGeoffrey's Satyrs and Epigrames. These were on the Lady Penelope Clifton, and on 'the death of the three sonnes of the Lord Sheffield, drowned neere where Trent falleth into Humber'. Neither is remarkable save for far-fetched conceits; they were reprinted in 1610, and again, with many others, in the volume of 1627. In 1619 Drayton issued a folio collected edition of his works, and reprinted it in 1620. In 1627 followed a folio of wholly fresh matter, including the Battaile of Agincourt; the Miseries of Queene Margarite, Nimphidia, Quest of Cinthia, Shepheards Sirena, Moone-Calfe, and Elegies upon sundry occasions. The Battaile of Agincourt is a somewhat otiose expansion, with purple patches, of the Ballad; it is, nevertheless, Drayton's best lengthy piece on a historical theme. Of the Miseries of Queene Margarite and of the Moone-Calfe we have already spoken. The most notable piece in the book is the Nimphidia. This poem of the Court of Fairy has 'invention, grace, and humour', as Canon Beeching has said. It would be interesting to know exactly when it was composed and committed to paper, for it is thought that the three fairy poems in Herrick's Hesperides were written about 1626. In any case, Drayton's poem touches very little, and chiefly in the beginning, on the subject of any one of Herrick's three pieces. The style, execution, and impression left on the reader are quite different; even as they are totally unlike those of the Midsummer Night's Dream. Herrick's pieces are extraordinary combinations of the idea of 'King of Shadows', with a reality fantastically sober: the poems are steeped in moonlight. In Drayton all is clear day, or the most unromantic of nights; though everything is charming, there is no attempt at idealization, little of the higher faculty of imagination; but great realism, and much play of fancy. Herrick's verses were written by Cobweb and Moth together, Drayton's by Puck. Granting, however, the initial deficiency in subtlety of charm, the whole poem is inimitably graceful and piquant. The gay humour, the demure horror of the witchcraft, the terrible seriousness of the battle, wonderfully realize the mock-heroic gigantesque; and while there is not the minute accuracy of Gulliver in Lilliput, Drayton did not write for a sceptical or too-prying audience; quite half his readers believed more or less in fairies. In the metre of the poem Drayton again echoes that of the older romances, as he did in Dowsabel. In the Quest of Cinthia, while ostensibly we come to the real world of mortals, we are really in a non-existent land of pastoral convention, in the most pseudo-Arcadian atmosphere in which Drayton ever worked. The metre and the language are, however, charmingly managed. The Shepheards Sirena is a poem, apparently, 'where more is meant than meets the ear,' as so often in pastoral poetry; it is difficult to see exactly what is meant; but the Jacobean strain of doubt and fear is there, and the poem would seem to have been written some time earlier than 1627. The Elegies comprise a great variety of styles and themes; some are really threnodies, some verse-letters, some laments over the evil times, and one a summary of Drayton's literary opinions. He employs the couplet in his Elegies with a masterly hand, often with a deliberately rugged effect, as in his broader Marstonic satire addressed to William Browne; while the line of greater smoothness but equal strength is to be seen in the letters to Sandys and Jeffreys. He is fantastic and conceited in most of the threnodies; but, as is natural, that on his old friend, Sir Henry Raynsford, is least artificial and fullest of true feeling. The epistle to Henery Reynolds. Of Poets and Poesie shows Drayton as a sane and sagacious critic, ready to see the good, but keen to discern the weakness also; perhaps the clearest evidence of his critical skill is the way in which nearly all of his judgements on his contemporaries coincide with the received modern opinions.

In his later years Drayton enjoyed the patronage of the third Earl and Countess of Dorset; and in 1630 he published his last volume, the Muses Elizium, of which he dedicated the pastoral part to the Earl, and the three divine poems at the end to the Countess. The Muses Elizium proper consists of Ten Pastorals or Nymphals, prefaced by a Description of Elizium. The three divine poems have been mentioned before, and were Noah's Floud, Moses his Birth and Miracles, and David and Goliah. The Nymphals are the crown and summary of much of the best in Drayton's work. Here he departed from the conventional type of pastoral, even more than in the Shepherd's Garland; but to say that he sang of English rustic life would hardly be true: the sixth Nymphal, allowing for a few pardonable exaggerations by the competitors, is almost all English, if we except the names; so is the tenth with the same exception; the first and fourth might take place anywhere, but are not likely in any country; the second is more conventional; the fifth is almost, but not quite, English; the third, seventh, and ninth are avowedly classical in theme; while the eighth is a more delicate and subtle fairy poem than the Nymphidia. The fourth and tenth Nymphals are also touched with the sadder, almost satiric vein; the former inveighing against the English imitation of foreigners and love of extravagance in dress; while the tenth complains simple often, sensuous rarely. His great industry, his careful study, and his great receptivity are shown in the unusual spectacle of a man who has sung well in the language of his youth, suddenly learning, in his age, the tongue spoken by the younger generation, and reproducing it with individuality and sureness of touch. It is in rhetoric, splendid or rugged, in argument, in plain statement or description, in the outline sketch of a picture, that Drayton excels; magic of atmosphere and colouring are rarely present. Stolidity is, perhaps, his besetting sin; yet it is the sign of a slow, not a dull, intellect; an intellect, like his heart, which never let slip what it had once taken to itself.

As a man Drayton would seem to have been an excellent type of the sturdy, clear-headed, but yet romantic and enthusiastic Englishman; gifted with much natural ability, sedulously increased by study; quietly humorous, self-restrained; and if temporarily soured by disappointment and the disjointed times, yet emerging at last into a greater serenity, a more unadulterated gaiety than had ever before characterized him. It is possible, but from his clear and sane balance of mind improbable, that many of his light later poems are due to deliberate self-blinding and self-deception, a walking in enchanted lands of the mind.

Of Drayton's three known portraits the earliest shows him at the age of thirty-six, and is now in the National Portrait Gallery. A look of quiet, speculative melancholy seems to pervade it; there is, as yet, no moroseness, no evidence of severe conflict with the world, no shadow of stress or of doubt. The second and best-known portrait shows us Drayton at the age of fifty, and was engraved by Hole, as a frontispiece to the poems of 1619. Here a notable change has come over the face; the mouth is hardened, and depressed at the corners through disappointment and disillusionment; the eyes are full of a pathos increased by the puzzled and perturbed uplift of the brows. Yet a stubbornness and tenacity of purpose invests the features and reminds us that Drayton is of the old and sound Elizabethan stock, 'on evil days though fallen.' Let it be remembered, that he was in 1613, when the portrait was taken, in more or less prosperous circumstances; it was the sad degeneracy, the meanness and feebleness of the generation around him, that chiefly depressed and embittered him. The final portrait, now in the Dulwich Gallery, represents the poet as a man of sixty-five; and is quite in keeping with the sunnier and calmer tone of his later poetry. It is the face of one who has not emerged unscathed from the world's conflict, but has attained to a certain calm, a measure of tranquillity, a portion of content, who has learnt the lesson that there is a soul of goodness in things evil. The Hole portrait shows him with long hair, small 'goatee' beard, and aquiline nose drawn up at the nostrils: while the National portrait shows a type of nose and beard intermediate between the Hole and the Dulwich pictures: the general contour of the face, though the forehead is broad enough, is long and oval. Drayton seems to have been tall and thin, and to have been very susceptible of cold, and therefore to have hated Winter and the North. He is said to have shared in the supper which caused Shakespeare's death; but his own verses breathe the spirit of Milton's sonnet to Cyriack Skinner, rather than that of a devotee of Bacchus.

He died in 1631, probably December 23, and was buried under the North wall of Westminster Abbey. Meres's opinion of his character during his early life is as follows: 'As Aulus Persius Flaccus is reported among al writers to be of an honest life and vpright conuersation: so Michael Drayton, quem totics honoris et amoris causa nomino, among schollers, souldiours, Poets, and all sorts of people is helde for a man of uertuous disposition, honest conversation, and well gouerned cariage; which is almost miraculous among good wits in these declining and corrupt times, when there is nothing but rogery in villanous man, and when cheating and craftines is counted the cleanest wit, and soundest wisedome.' Fuller also, in a similar strain, says, 'He was a pious poet, his conscience having the command of his fancy, very temperate in his life, slow of speech, and inoffensive in company.'

of the improvident and wasteful felling of trees in the English forests. This last Nymphal, though designedly an epilogue, is probably rather a warning than a despairing lament, even though we conceive the old satyr to be Drayton himself. As a whole the Nymphals show Drayton at his happiest and lightest in style and metre; at his moments of greatest serenity and even gaiety; an atmosphere of sunshine seems to envelope them all, though the sun sink behind a cloud in the last. His music now is that of a rippling stream, whereas in his earlier days he spoke weightier and more sonorous words, with a mouth of gold.

To estimate the poetical faculty of Drayton is a somewhat perplexing task; for, while rarely subtle, or rising to empyrean heights, he wrote in such varied styles, on such various themes, that the task, at first, seems that of criticizing many poets, not one. But through all his work runs the same eminently English spirit, the same honesty and clearness of idea, the same stolidity of purpose, and not infrequently of execution also; the same enthusiasm characterizes all his earlier, and much of his later work; the enthusiasm especially characteristic of Elizabethan England, and shown by Drayton in his passion for England and the English, in his triumphant joy in their splendid past, and his certainty of their future glory. As a poet, he lacked imagination and fine fury; he supplied their place by the airiest and clearest of fancies, by the strenuous labour of a great brain illumined by the steady flame of love for his country and for his lady. Mr. Courthope has said that he lacked loftiness and resolution of artistic purpose; without these, we ask, how could a man, not lavishly dowered with poetry in his soul, have achieved so much of it? It was his very fixity and loftiness of purpose, his English stubbornness and doggedness of resolution that enabled him to surmount so many obstacles of style and metre, of subject and thought. His two purposes, of glorifying his mistress and his friends, and of sounding England's glories past and future, while insisting on the dangers of a present decadence, never flagged or failed. All his poetry up to 1627 has this object directly or secondarily; and much after this date. Of the more abstract and universal aspects of his art he had not much conception; but he caught eagerly at the fashionable belief in the eternizing power of poetry; and had it not been that, where his patriotism was uppermost, he was deficient in humour and sense of proportion, he would have succeeded better: as it is, his more directly patriotic pieces are usually the dullest or longest of his works. He requires, like all other poets, the impulse of an absolutely personal and individual feeling, a moment of more intimate sympathy, to rouse him to his heights of song. Thus the Ballad of Agincourt is on the very theme of all patriotic themes that most attracted him; Virginian and other Voyages lay very close to his heart; and in certain sonnets to his lady lies his only imperishable work. Of sheer melody and power of song he had little, apart from his themes: he could not have sat down and written a few lark's or nightingale's notes about nothing as some of his contemporaries were able to do: he required the stimulus of a subject, and if he were really moved thereby he beat the music out. Only in one or two of the later Odes, and in the volumes of 1627 and 1630, does his music ever seem to flow from him naturally. Akin to this quality of broad and extensive workmanship, to this faculty of taking a subject and when writing, with all thought concentrated on it, rather than on the method of writing about it, is his strange lack of what are usually called 'quotations'. For this is not only due to the fact that he is little known; there are, besides, so few detached remarks or aphorisms that are separately quotable; so few examples of that curiosa felicitas of diction: lines like these,

Thy Bowe, halfe broke, is peec'd with old desire;
Her Bowe is beauty with ten thousand strings....

are rare enough. Drayton, in fact, comes as near controverting the statement Poeta nascitur, non fit, as any one in English literature: by diligent toil and earnest desire he won a place for himself in the second rank of English poets: through love he once set foot in the circle of the mightiest. Sincere he was always,

A Chronology of Michael Drayton's Life and Works

1563	Drayton born at Hartshill, Warwickshire.
c. 1572	Drayton a page in the house of Sir Henry Goodere, at Polesworth.
c. 1574	Anne Goodere born
February, 1591	Drayton in London. Harmony of Church.
1593	Idea, the Shepherd's Garland. Legend of Peirs Gaveston.
1594	Ideas Mirrour. Matilda. Lucy Harrington becomes Countess of Bedford.
1595	Sir Henry Goodere the elder dies. Endimion and Phoebe, dedicated to Lucy Bedford.
1595-6	Anne Goodere married to Sir Henry Raynsford.
1596	Mortimeriados. Legends of Robert, Matilda, and Gaveston.
1597	England's Heroical Epistles.
1598	Drayton already at work on the Poly-Olbion.
1599	Epistles and Idea sonnets, new edition. (Date of Drayton portrait in National Portrait Gallery.)
1600	Sir John Oldcastle.
1602	New edition of Epistles and Idea.
1603	Drayton made an Esquire of the Bath, to Sir Walter Aston. To the Maiestie of King James. Barons' Wars.
1604	The Owle. A Pean Triumphall. Moyses in a Map of his Miracles.
1605	First collected edition of Poems. Another edition of Idea and Epistles.
1606	Poemes Lyrick and Pastorall. Odes. Eglogs. The Man in the Moone.
1607	Legend of Great Cromwell.
1608	Reprint of Collected Poems.
1609	Another edition of Cromwell.
1610	Reprint of Collected Poems.
1613	Reprint of Collected Poems. First Part of Poly-Olbion.
1618	Two Elegies in FitzGeoffrey's Satyrs and Epigrames.
1619	Collected Folio edition of Poems.
1620	Second edition of Elegies, and reprint of 1619 Poems.
1622	Poly-Olbion complete.
1627	Battle of Agincourt, Nymphidia, &c.
1630	Muses Elizium. Noah's Floud. Moses his Birth and Miracles. David and Goliah.
1631	Second edition of 1627 folio. Drayton dies December 23rd.
1636	Posthumous poem appeared in Annalia Dubrensia.
1637	Poems.

Michael Drayton – A Concise Bibliography

The Major Works

The Harmony of the Church (1591)
Idea, The Shepherd's Garland (1593)
Idea's Mirror (1594)

Peirs Gaveston (1593 or 1594)
Matilda (1594)
Endimion and Phoebe: Idea's Latmus (1595)
The Tragical Legend of Robert, Duke of Normandy (1596)
Mortimeriados (1596)
England's Heroicall Epistles (1597)
The First Part of the Life of Sir John Oldcastle (1600)
The Barons' Wars in the Reign of Edward II (1603)
The Owl (1604)
The Man in the Moon (1606)
The Legend of Thomas Cromwell, Earl of Essex (1607)
Poly-Olbion (1612 & 1622)
Idea (1619)
Pastorals: Containing Eclogues (1619)
Odes (1619)
The Battle of Agincourt (published 1627)
The Quest of Cynthia (published 1627)
Elegies Upon Sundry Occasions (1627)
Nymphidia, the Court of Fairy (1627)
The Shepherd's Sirena (1627)
Muses' Elysium (1630)
Moses' Birth and Miracles (1630)